BETTER LEFT SAID

DIARY OF A SINGLE GIRL TURNED CHRISTIAN

AMBER RHODES

Allure Charm Events LLC
Tucker, Georgia

BETTER LEFT SAID
DIARY OF A SINGLE GIRL TURNED CHRISTIAN

Allure Charm Events LLC
Tucker, Georgia 30084

ISBN 978-0-692-90527-2

Manufactured in the United States of America
First printing June 2017

Dedication

To my husband for pushing me closer to the heart of God, to my Dallas for keeping me joyful, to my sisters, brother, parents, pastors, church family and friends for believing in what God is doing in my life, and for every single girl who truly wants freedom but doesn't know how - this book is dedicated to you.

TABLE OF CONTENTS

PREFACE

What doesn't kill you, makes you stronger.

These are the words that resonate in my heart: time after time. And I was plainly sick of being *sick and tired*. You've heard that before, right? Well, it holds true when you know – *and feel* – what it means.

I was the type of girl that thought I could save a man. *Gullible* perhaps, but I really thought if I did the best I could for my boyfriend, and I was true and faithful only to him, in return he would be good to me, stay faithful to me, and not cheat. Women, why do we want a bad guy who's only good to us? I mean I laugh even when writing that because it sounds ridiculous. I want a *good* bad guy. I want a *soft* thug. I want a *hard* pretty boy. That sounds stupid! But I really thought I could save a man, and that is just one thing you cannot do. Trying to save a man *who doesn't want to be saved* is as stupid as pulling a stubborn horse to water who's not thirsty.

But I was she. I was her. Because any relationship I was involved in, I loved them to the greatest potential I could. And I found that if I did and he saw that I was a good girl, he would surely want to stay with me, and want to be with me, and only me, for the rest of our lives. I mean, this is the formula for a guy's affection, right?

WRONG.

CAMRON

"Hey, let me talk to you for a minute!" this guy said to me coming out of the gymnasium. The probate was over and the festivities calmed down. I walked out with my friends and on the way to the car and this guy, who just crossed over into the prestigious fraternity, approached me.

"Can I get your number?" he asked.

"And your name is?" I questioned.

"Camron...and I be seeing you around sometimes. I couldn't approach you when I wanted to, but I see you now, and I want to get to know you." He had that cocky smile. That smile like *you can't say no* smile. The smile as in *I just crossed the prestigious fraternity, and I dare you say no* type of smile. So I smiled and gave him my number. I actually felt a little privileged that he wanted to talk to me. I was hesitant, however, to do so as well. I mean, I was involved with two of his big brothers in the fraternity. I wasn't sure if my reputation preceded me, but I didn't care. Those were over and done with. I walked on to my friends car and spilled the beans, as we drove back to the campus apartments.

I didn't hear from him that much. I mean a few calls, maybe. But then, two months later, he invited me to a Valentine's Day ball his fraternity was hosting, which I declined to go to. He invited me to his campus apartment on many occasions, at night, which I also declined but probably twice. One time I came over there to spend the night with him, but nothing sexual happened. He made it no better for me to be there by lighting candles and trying to drip hot wax on me. I was so uncomfortable that in the middle of the night I opted to go back to my apartment. The other time was when I went over there and saw some girls' underwear pinned up over his bed. And I didn't want to bring it up, but I asked him about the panties that were on the wall staring at me. His response was, "I ain't even going to lie, that is Tracy's underwear. She wanted them pinned up over my bed when we…you know…" I was so shocked he was honest with me, and knowing I knew Tracy at that. And on that note, I exited his apartment.

As you can tell, he kept peeping his head in and out of my life for an entire year. I didn't take him seriously at all. I didn't think he was that serious about me, but every time I thought that, there he was checking in on me again. He visited me when I was in summer school, but not until our college homecoming that year, he finally took me out on a real date. He told me to "give him a chance."

We went to the Shrimp Factory on River Street in Savannah. We talked about school, about people, about life, and about "us." I told him I didn't think he was serious. He told me he was and wanted to be with me.

"Listen Nikki," – that's what he called me when he was serious – "I know what I want. I know I want to be with you. Forget what anyone has said about me. I will forget what everyone says about you. And let's just do this thing."

I just couldn't make the decision at that time, whether or not to believe him. I had enjoyed the date. Despite a lot of opposition from my girlfriends to not go out with Camron, I was surprised at how good of a time I had with him.

A little over a month later, after talking to him almost every day, I called him up. By that time, he had went back to Florida where he stayed because he didn't attend college anymore.

"Ok, Camron," I said, "I believe you. I thought about it, and I want to be yours."

"Are you sure, Nikki?"

I told him, yes. Yes, I wanted to be his girlfriend. Yes I wanted to be with him. Just like that, we were together. And I was happy. A couple of weeks later, Camron came up from Florida to visit me. I was scheduled to work over the Christmas holiday, so I stayed in Savannah during our Christmas break. And he kept me company for a couple of days until I was able to hit the road to go home to Atlanta for New Year's.

Over that time during the break, he told me he wanted some TV's for his headrests in his car. I was sensing he wanted me to get them, but I told him I didn't have money to get them because they were more than a thousand dollars. I had nowhere near that amount in my bank. I told him if that is what he wanted, I would help him get them with whatever I had, and he reluctantly said, "That will do." So I gave over half of what I had for his Christmas present, and went to his bank to transfer the money in his account. I felt I shouldn't have done this for him, but I was so infatuated with him, so I wanted to help him out.

Valentine's week came. Camron told me he had a meeting in Atlanta with a basketball coach for a local team. He had to meet with him about his future on the sub-league basketball team. I was excited for Camron! What an opportunity! I didn't like that I had to spend Valentine's Day alone, but he promised he would come right back the next day and take me to Hilton Head for shopping and a nice dinner. So the day arrived, and I wished him safe travels and well on his business trip. In turn, he left a box of chocolates and a balloon in my room before he hopped on his plane to Atlanta, while I was in my 7 o'clock class that morning. When he got to Atlanta, of course he called, and we chatted briefly before he had his meeting. I didn't hear from him for the rest of Valentine's Day.

The next day I was super excited and anxious to see him. I went to pick him up from the airport, and we came back to my apartment so he could change from his travel sweats. From there, we went to Hilton Head, going from store to store, buying and spending. I was excited! This was the type of stuff you saw only in the movies, and I was living it! I felt lucky to be his! We ate an Italian dinner that evening, and then we went back to my apartment for the rest of the night. Yes, this totally made up for missing the actual Valentine's day.

Then came suspicion – suspicion that he was cheating and entertaining other girls. He was taking calls in the other rooms when we were together. There were nights where he didn't come back to my place while he was in Savannah. There were actual girls coming to my face and telling me what they did together. This sickened me. Worry kept me up at night, crying. Even my roommate heard me crying in my room at nights. She told me, "Amber, I'm tired of hearing that. You have to do better." Worry about what he was doing while I wasn't with him kept me from having an appetite. I felt like I had to know where he was at all times for me to be secure. The lies then started soon thereafter: "I was just hanging with frat"; "I was just getting my hair cut"; "I needed some alone time." Those excuses wore me out to the point of losing weight and my hair shedding.

I will never forget this one time…

"So you are just going to leave me here alone for spring break by myself?" I asked, as he was packing up to leave.

"I told my mom in Philly I was coming to see her, what you want me to do?" he asked sarcastically, and with that same sly grin and chuckle, brushing off my feelings.

"I mean, I wanted us to do some things, ya know?"

"I'm only gone for a few days, and I will be right back." He leaned over to kiss me, as we began to walk out the apartment.

"Aye bruh!" his fraternity brother called to from the car outside, "You ready to get to Miami?" Now I am very sure his fraternity brother just ruined his secret of really going to Miami instead of Philadelphia. My back was turned to Camron, as I was looking puzzled at his friend in the car down the steps. I could feel Camron gesturing to the guy to *hush* right behind me. I turned around, pretending not to hear, and kissed my guy and said, "Have a great time in Philly." I left the house and returned to my apartment, in disbelief of the lies, again.

Later that week, he called and told me how his mom was doing in Philadelphia. He even put a girl on the phone pretending to be his sister to chat with me for a minute. He told me he loved me, and he'd be back soon. Upon returning back to Savannah, I saw some male enhancement pills in his car I've never seen before. I asked him what these were for? He lied about those, explaining those were his friends pills and not his.

But I stayed in the relationship. I stayed with a liar. I stayed with a cheater. Because I loved him.

Approaching graduation, Camron got no better. We had some great days, but most of the time was our arguing. We made up but then argued some more. That was my life with him for the four months we were together. The night before my graduation day, I didn't see him or hear from him. I assumed he was with some other girl. So my roommate and a couple of my sorority sisters went out and celebrated our 'big day' that was to come the next day. They asked if I wanted to go, but I just wanted Camron to surprise me and call me. Of course he didn't.

Within the following days after graduation, we took a trip down to Jacksonville. He wanted to take me to Jacksonville as a gift for graduation. We rode down, making frequent stops for him to "use the restroom," but I suspected he was making his calls to his other girls. When we got to the hotel, he stepped out the room to make more calls. By this time, I really had enough. I was tired. I was really tired. Of the lies, of the worry, of the anxiety, of the stress. I was tired from it all. The next day, I wanted to leave. We were to stay for a few days, but I didn't want to stay any more days with him. He obliged, upset at the "dummy trip" we made, and we rode back in silence, two hours straight, back up to Savannah. From there, I left Savannah for Atlanta.

***

"Hello, did someone just call my house?" said a woman on the other side of the phone.

"Yes, I'm calling to speak to Camron," I said.

"Well Camron isn't here. He left. And this is his fiancée, and I am down here with him. He asked me, in front of his mom and family last night for me to be his wife, so I accepted his proposal. I am surprised he even gave a chick his house phone number. Normally he don't give this one out. Anyway don't call here again!" And she hung up the phone in my face.

I was raging mad. Not even a month leaving Savannah, Camron proposed? My heart sunk so low. "*Why did I take him back?*" I kept asking myself dialing and re-dialing his cell phone number. He finally answered.

"What do you want!?" he screamed at me over the receiver

"So you have a fiancé now, Camron?" I asked with a shaky crying, desperate voice.

"See, I told you not to call that number until an emergency. I don't want to talk about it with you." And he hung up the phone in my face. I never felt so alone, as I did in that moment. With shaky hands and the cringe in my stomach, I kept calling him and kept calling him, but it was no answer on his end. I didn't know what to do! I went outside my mom's house and walked up the street and back down again, trying to calm myself down. I could not be a nervous wreck when my mom got home, so I seriously tried everything in my power to keep from bawling crying again. I stayed in my room for the rest of the night, with short word answers to my mom, and pretending I didn't want the phone to ring.

12:45 am. The phone rings. It's Camron. Half sleep I answer the phone, "What?"

"Listen babe. I'm sorry. I didn't know what to tell you at first. I am not her fiancé. She crazy. I did not propose to her last night. She wants me back, and I brought her down here to Florida because I wanted to tell her face to face that I didn't want her anymore. I just want you. I'm sorry she said those things, but I don't want her."

I tried so hard not to burst out in tears, and the only thing I could muster up to say was, "Goodnight."

The next few months I was off and on with Camron. I really couldn't be "all the way" committed to him knowing he was not in Atlanta. He came to visit, but there was no way possible I could call him my boyfriend again. Even one of my sorority sisters called me to tell me she, too, was talking to him. I just couldn't take the crap anymore from him. I was in Georgia. He was in Florida. We even met up at our college homecoming later that year, against my best friends wishes, and hung out a little with him before we went to the bar that evening. Stupidly, I ended up right back in his bed at the end of that night.

He moved up to Atlanta for a little bit. He rented a townhome in the south side of town where we then, started our relationship over. But I didn't fully trust him. I couldn't fully trust him. Over and over again, I would ask myself *why I was in this relationship if I didn't trust him?* But I thought I loved him, and that is what love is. Love looks over the things done wrong to it. Love forgives. Love keeps on pressing.

However, we still had arguments. He still lied and cheated, so it didn't last very long for me to move on. Actually I got a little help....

CHARLES

"Hey, welcome to Ruby Tuesday! I'm Amber, and I'll be taking great care of you tonight!" I smiled. "Can I start you off with something to drink?" I looked at both the mother and son just seated by the hostess in my section.

"Yeah we celebrating tonight! She just bought a house! I just bought a house! We celebrating! Give me a Long Island!" the son excitingly exclaimed.

I didn't know if I was ready for the energy he offered that slow Wednesday night. "OK sir," I laughed. "And for you ma'am?"

"Give me the same thing," she said, smirking at her son.

I checked on the table every now and then, as usual, giving my best to each table that comes into my section. Every time I came to the table to check on the two, the son would look very deep into my eyes, not quite sure if he was flirting or if he offered intensity along with his energy. When it was time for the bill, the mom pulled out her wallet, but he beat her to it by offering me his card. "Here you go, Miss Ruby," he said as he gave me his credit card to pay. I smiled again – *it wasn't like I get that treatment from customers like that often.*

As I walked away, he mumbled loud enough for me to hear, "And when you bring me back my receipt to sign, make sure your number on there." I took note of his appearance; he was a cute brown skinned, slender fella with a creole country accent that melted my heart. I was so used to Southern accents from Atlanta, it was refreshing to hear someone new. One thing I noted – He took care of his mom, which you didn't find often. Seeing them interact at the table while I was serving on them confirmed he really appreciated his mom, and had a very close relationship with her.

"Oh I see you did it, huh? My name Charles by the way," he said as I brought the receipt back to him with his credit card. His mom already had made her way to the restroom.

"I did. Use it," I said with a grin, as his mom returned from the restroom. "OK, y'all. Have a good night." I smiled to her then to him. As I was turning to walk away, excited to tell the girls in the back the news, I could tell his eyes followed me until I left his sight.

***

"Hey, this Amber?" a familiar voice said on the receiver of my phone as I was driving back home from my sister's house.

"Yes, this is her." I automatically assumed this was Charles, even though it was about two weeks later from when I met him. I didn't give my number out that much and it was the familiar accent and energy that really gave it away. "Charles?" I asked.

"Well it better be!" He laughed. We had a brief conversation, mainly because he was on his way to his mom's new home to put up some blinds in her windows and door panels. From that first conversation, he seemed so simple and easy going. He wasn't at all nervous about talking to me, even though I was surprisingly nervous about him. He ended the conversation and told me he was going to call me back later that night when he was finished.

I didn't hear from him until three days later.

Then, we talked consistently. By this time, this was the end of 2009. We text and called each other constantly. He came over to hang out in my apartment, and I came over to his house from time to time to chill and watch movies. Entering into the next year, he helped me move from my studio apartment in midtown, to my one bedroom apartment a little bit north of the city. Since it was only a studio I was moving from, he packed up everything I had in a trailer hooked to the back of his Chevy Suburban and moved everything in. So what better way to thank him than to cook him a nice dinner, Chicken Marsala, and a relaxing night with me on Valentine's weekend?

"You didn't have to do all of this for me, Ruby!" I could tell he was excited as he entered into my apartment smelling the aroma of the marsala chicken.

"Well you know I had to repay you for moving me in." I took his coat, invited him to the couch to watch TV until the dinner was ready. Salad, chicken marsala, garlic bread was prepared for him. I wore my tight black dress, with my hair flowing down just above my shoulders and my black peep toe heels. After serving him, we watched the movie *Love Jones*, one of my favorite love stories. As we finished, Charles wondered if he could stay the night, and I told him he could.

The next morning was Valentine's Day, which was on a Sunday. I got up and made breakfast for him, gave him his "beer basket" I made out of Coronas for his Valentine's gift, and thanked him for coming over and spending time with me. He stuck around until about noon that day because he had to go home and take care of his dog and run some errands. He thanked me again for such a good date night and we would catch up later that evening.

Throughout the year, Charles and I were "together" even though we never made anything official. I would drive over to his house some nights spend the night and take off to work the next morning. Some nights he would do the same over my apartment. I cooked for him some times, and let me try his famous recipes the other times. We were comfortable. I had no reason to think he would cheat. He had no time to cheat. From his parcel service job, he would get off around eight or nine each day then call me right after until he got home and in bed. He would frequently call me at work in the mornings, to tell me how his day is going, or how crazy his morning was. I was pleased with him, but I just felt odd that I really didn't have a title with him. His mom loved me, his friends loved me (one even tried to *talk* to me), and I could tell he really liked me and my company. We became friends more than anything because of how respected I felt while I was with him. He even came to my rescue after work one evening to help me move from that apartment to my mom's house because of the rat infestation that was going on, and I had to move quick! Another time, for a week, I went to get him in the morning (or I spent the night over his house) to drive him to work because he rear ended a lady one morning with his Suburban, and totaled her car and his!

One Saturday morning, after a night that Charles and I enjoyed together at a club, he woke up to go to his usual Saturday morning barber appointment. He left me there so I could get some more sleep, which shocked me that he trust me there with his pit bull, named Deuce, walking around playing. So I slept a little more until he came back. Once he did, I got myself up and dressed, and we went out that Saturday morning to run errands. *I was superexcited, even though I didn't show any signs of it. We were acting like a couple and doing couple things! This was a milestone in our relationship for me. It felt good to be with a street boy who wanted only me.* When we was out running errands, we were stopped by the police. His car reeked of marijuana, and I am assuming the cops pulled him over because of it. So we pulled into a local breakfast place, and the officers came to the car to see what was going on inside the car. Charles also admitted to his registered gun inside the car, too. But the officers didn't find any drugs on him, so they let us go.

"Man I am so glad you were with me," Charles said laughing.

"Why is that?" I asked as we sat in the car for a minute.

"Man, if you wouldn't have been in this car, they probably would have took me still, even though I didn't have nothing in the car," he said.

I didn't know the technicalities of what an officer can and cannot do, but I was thankful that the cops didn't arrest him! I wouldn't know what to do! After that incident, we got some breakfast and headed back to his house. That was my first adventure of any kind like that, and it didn't frighten me at all. But it did give me more of a love for him. *Don't ask me why.*

Later that year, when my birthday was around the corner, my family was planning a trip to the cabins, and I of course wanted Charles to be my friend to come along with me. So I told him about it two months prior if he was interested, which he was. He didn't get to do things like that, so he was excited about it. We would go a week after my birthday to the cabins.

But then on my birthday, Charles called me after he got off of work. "Hey man, what you doing?" he said. I really couldn't believe I accepted his call.

"I'm good," I short answered him back.

"That's what up. You all right?"

"I mean, yeah," I replied.

"You sure?" he asked.

"My birthday Charles. My birthday," I told him, trying not to burst out in tears of frustration.

"Oh, dang. That's today huh? Man."

"Yep. So I'm going to get off the phone now," I said. I really didn't want to talk to him.

I guess he understood because all he told me was "Ok, I'll talk to you later," which frustrated me more.

He did, however, call me back that night apologizing that he missed saying "Happy birthday" to me explaining again that he was really bad with birthdays. I even talked to him earlier that day at work, and he didn't mention it. But I gave him the entire day to get it right, and he didn't. I really couldn't believe it, and I really didn't want him to come on the trip knowing I would still be upset about it.

"So, you don't want me to go now?" he said.

"Not really," I told him. "I just know how I am, and I don't want to have to fake the funk around my family with you pretending everything is ok when it isn't, knowing I am mad."

"I mean, I understand, that's how you feel." Charles was always a nonchalant type person. He wasn't going to beg. He wouldn't let you in sometimes, but he had subtle things he would say or how he would say it if he cared. This was one of those moments where I could tell he really wanted to go, but wasn't going to beg to go. But I actually didn't want him to go to the cabins with us anymore. "Sorry I missed your birthday," he said, and we ended the call.

***

New Year's Eve that year came. I went out with my girls to a party that was at Atlanta Turner Field. It was going to be great music, free flowing champagne and bar drinks, food and fireworks. Well, most of that was true, but the party was one of the best I had been in a very long time. I was supposed to see Charles before I went out, but that didn't happen. He wanted to see what I looked like before I left, but his sense of timing was off that night because he had to work. He could never give me a definite time for anything. But that night, he got off work later than he expected, so I didn't see him before I went to my friend's house on the north side of town.

"Yeah, I probably won't be going anywhere tonight," he told me over the phone, as I was on my way to my friend's house. "Steve is having this thing at his house, and I don't really want to go. I'm super tired. I'm just probably going to chill and drink some Hennessey."

"Oh, OK. Well, once we leave, I'll be making my way to you, that's ok?" I asked. He said it was fine.

My girls and I had a great time at the party. Even though food was slim, it was made up by the heavy alcoholic drinks the bartenders made. We partied hard. After the party and countdown, around 12:30 I called Charles. "Hey, I'm on my way to you from downtown."

"Well I'm not home. I ended up going to Steve's house."

"OK, so are you leaving?"

"Not really. I mean, not right now. Where you headed?"

Frustrated I said, "Well I was headed over there to you, but since you aren't home then I'll go back home!"

"Well I can call you when I leave."

"No, that's OK," I was even more upset. "Once I'm in my mother's house and set her alarm, I'm not going back out. But have a good night, Charles." I ended the call. I was so upset! I mean, really upset. We had a plan. I thought I was going to at least spend time with my boo that night, yet he was over Steve's house and didn't want to leave? I continued to zoom down Highway 20 to my mom's house. Angry, I turned in for the night and turned off my phone.

The next day, I didn't call or text Charles. And while I was waiting for his call to me, my family went to my big sister's house to eat fried fish and collard greens, a new year's tradition. Then he called.

"So I guess I wasn't going to talk to you today?" he asked curious.

"I mean I am still upset how you did me last night, but it's whatever, Charles."

"So I want to see you. Can you come over?"

"I don't think so. But I'll talk to you tomorrow." We ended the call. In my mind, I couldn't deal with this any longer. The fact that I really couldn't get upset with him because we were not yet "official" killed me. I didn't know where I stood with him. And I desperately wanted to find out. On my way home I called him back, and he answered.

"Look, I need to know where I stand with you," I said. "We have been together for almost a year now, and I'm upset because I can't really get upset with you because I don't know who I am to you. It's like, do I even have a right to be upset with you? Where do I stand?"

"Listen, you are a good girl. You good, good to me and everything. But I don't see myself being with anyone right now."

My heart sunk. "Well, OK then. We don't need to be 'together' doing stuff together, as like we are a couple but not. Charles, I like you a lot, as you can tell. And I can't continue to do what we been doing and you not make me official."

"So you giving me an ultimatum?"

"Realistically, yes, I am. I need to know if you want to be with me or not?"

"Well, Amber, I just can't do that with you right now." My heart sunk more. "And I respect that you have to do what you have to do."

"Goodbye Charles." I ended the phone call as I approached my mother's house. I wanted to cry, but I couldn't. I had to be cool. I had to be strong. I had to see it for what it was and what he told me. As bad as it hurt, he was brutally honest with me. He didn't want to be with anyone right then. I had to suck up my feelings and continue on. But even after that night, with his birthday two days away, I still managed to bring him his gift and leave it on his car that night. I couldn't look him in the face, but wanted to at least be kind in that way. He called me to tell me he appreciated the gesture.

Within a few weeks, I moved into my new apartment on the north side of town. I couldn't help but constantly think about Charles. But what got me through the heartbreak was Destiny's Child, Beyoncé and Keri Hilson songs. I played them in my car on the way to and from work. I just couldn't believe I gave Charles all of me – my emotions, my body, my mind –everything about me for him to not appreciate and want me back in that capacity. I felt so foolish. I felt dumb, and felt the time was totally wasted with him.

But the hurt feelings didn't stop there.

I was still his friend on social media. One particular post on his page really bothered me – he was very close to one girl on his picture he posted. I wondered as I searched his page, *"How is he friends with her? She went to my high school. How does he know her?"* She made comments under his posts suggesting how they were meeting up one particular night. And then, there was that punch in my gut. *So they talking now? Wow Charles? Really?* I was disgusted. I was even more disgusted with myself for the next move I made.

One night while on the town with one of my friends who came up to Atlanta that weekend, I decided to pay Charles a visit. *1:02 am. Yes, in the middle of the night.* I wanted to see what he was up to. Maybe he was just getting in, too? Maybe I could come and spend the night with him. Yes, these were drunken thoughts. Not tipsy but really drunken. As I approached his house, there was an unfamiliar car in the driveway. Rage took over me, hurt and tears. I immediately called him right away. With no answer on the fifth time, I decided against the next foolish move, to repeatedly knock on his door, and then just made my way back home.

"Man, what's up?" He called me back 30 minutes later. "You blowing up my phone and stuff. What's the problem?"

"What's the problem, Charles? So you spending the night with her now? So she over there?" I said, still slurring a bit. I did make it home safely, and I was on my couch still in my club clothes.

"Maaaaan, are you serious right now? This ain't none of your business. I can't believe you came over here. Where are you now?"

"I'm at home right now."

"Are you drunk?"

"Yes."

"Ruby, I'm about to get off the phone with you. Calling me in the middle of the night. Showing up at my doorstep. That ain't cool, and I told you I don't like that." He didn't hang up immediately. He waited until I said "Ok" to hang up. He was at least that much of a gentleman. I cried myself to sleep that night, in my club dress, with mascara running all over my couch. That cut very deep.

I didn't hear from Charles immediately after. I didn't want to. I understood completely where I stood with him, and I didn't have a standing in his life. I had a place, but it was kept up by another woman.

I honestly cared about Charles. Besides the fact he didn't want me to be his girlfriend, he was a great guy and a hard worker. That's what I loved most about him. But I felt used up and played by him, and he was on to the next one, which I couldn't believe.

TERRANCE

"So, I say we kick it tonight? What you think?" Terrance said walking out to the parking deck with me. "I promise, it'll change ya life." He said it with a slick grin.

"Uh, no thank you. I'm tired, and just ready to go home." We walked out of Ruby Tuesday after our shift. Terrance was a cook, and of course, I was a waitress. We both returned back to the Ruby Tuesday establishment the same time after leaving in the previous year or two. He was so obnoxious to me. He was the baby daddy of a girl I used to be cool with who used to work there also. But she left for California a year prior, and I assumed they were not together anymore. But he had a bad attitude, a nasty one. He always said some slick things to me that hurt because he was the type that disrespected women; I assumed this anyway by his potty mouth and "I don't care" attitude.

"All right, it'll change your life! I promise you." He looked me up and down as he began to smoke his cigarette.

"No thanks Terrance." I laughed, as I opened my car across the parking lot.

Within two or three weeks time after that, Terrance made little gestures and said some of the same things to me while we worked together, which was mostly on Friday and Saturday nights. I couldn't take him seriously. I mean, Terrance? The flirt? Weedhead? No.

But the more and more we talked, the more and more I liked him. I laughed a lot when I was at work with him. He clowned on people, which I thought was very funny, or maybe it was the boredom sometimes we worked against. We exchanged numbers and got more acquainted over the phone. The phone conversations went from 15 minutes to 30 minutes to hours. He would call to tell me about his day, and his troubles he was having with his roommate. I would share some of my stories to him. And as time progressed, I became more comfortable with him.

My birthday came! I was so excited. I invited a bunch of my friends to my birthday dinner at a Japanese steakhouse followed by an "after party" in my apartment. Earlier in the day, I went to the Dominican salon to get my hair pressed out and straightened. I went to buy about three or four bottles of liquor from the liquor store, with shot glasses and chasers. It was my 26th birthday. I wanted to do something I never done or had before.

"Well hey Ruby!" a familiar voice called me the day of my birthday. Charles. Oh, goodness.

"Well hey Charles. Nice to hear from you!"

"Happy Birthday…see I didn't forget!"

"Well I see!" I laughed. I told him what I was getting into for the day, and he didn't really want anything but to prove to me he remembered my birthday, so we got off the phone, and ended on good terms.

The next call I got was from Terrance. I told him again about my plans for my birthday and told him he was more than welcome to come to the after party. I gave him my address, and he said he would be there.

That night was great. I was surrounded by family and friends at the Japanese steakhouse, then my friends followed me to the "after party" at my apartment. There, we had music, spade games, and drinking games. Everyone was loud and having a good time. My co-workers from Ruby Tuesday were there as well, turning it all up just a notch. Then in walks Terrance. I was happy to see him.

He came in that night looking very, very fine with his regular jeans and polo tee with a vest. He stood 5 feet 9 inches tall, but his stature had swag that added to his personality. His dimples on his smooth light brown complexion is what really made me fall for him. He stayed to himself for the most part of the night but talked with the rest of the cooks from Ruby Tuesday that was there as well.

The night dwindled down, everyone who was left there had too much to drink, and everyone needed to go home. My friend Jasmin, who drove two hours to celebrate my birthday, of course, stayed the night with me. Everyone had to leave. It was almost 3 am! So, trying to keep my composure and stature, I greeted everyone out, showed everyone how to get out of the apartment and showed them to their cars. I told Terrance to hold tight so he could stay the night with me.

***

"You know I'm starting to feel close to you," Terrance started out one Saturday afternoon as we talked on the phone. I was lying in my bed, a typical day when I didn't have to work at Ruby Tuesday. "I'm trying to make sense of these feelings. Like am I feeling you? Yes. A lot. You so chill. You keep it real." My ears started to perk up. "And we been chillin together for a while. You know what I mean? It's just good with you."

I started to smile. But I knew in the back of my mind my agreement: I didn't want no relationship with him. At all. "So what you're saying," I began, "is **what,** Terrance?"

"I mean," he started to fumble over his words, "can it be official? Just you and me? Together? I really like you and I want to be with you."

I thought about it for a moment. Didn't think I would say, "Yes," but those words came out of my mouth to him. What world of trouble was I in to? Was I disloyal to the girl who I knew that used to date him, and had his baby? Was he serious? Was he just in his feelings? How were we going to "be together" at work? Was I ready for another relationship?

The next two months were November and December, which meant his birthday and Christmas. Terrance and I were steady and happy for those months at least. Nothing really troubled me about him, I was calm. Working two jobs, I had no option but to be calm! One more thing wasn't going to stress me out!! Within the first month, however, he let me know that he could possibly be the dad of a newborn baby girl. At the same time, his other baby mama had put him on child support, and it started to collect from his check. He was stressed. The Ruby Tuesday line cook job wasn't paying enough. I tried to keep him calm, doing what it was I could to help him in the situation. Then more bad news, someone hit his car head on while parked in the street in front of his mom's house. (It was a teenage driver going too fast around the curve to his moms neighborhood.) So he was out of a car! I couldn't believe all of this was happening to him, so fast! So, there were times where he would spend the night with me, and I would ride with my sister to work for him to use my car.

But besides all of that, *which looking at it hindsight I was out of my mind,* I enjoyed him! I enjoyed his daughter (from his first baby's mother), as she sometimes came over with him. She was a super angel, so sweet and innocent. I loved her! He lived a very simple life. Besides work, he would just like to chill, with me, with his friends, or just at his house. He didn't go out that much, even though we went to a bar or two while we were together. He just loved being over my place, watching movies, laughing, joking, cooking and eating. He would cook for me sometimes, and I would cook for him sometimes. That's how our relationship worked. And in that point in my life, I was fine with it. New Year's came and went. We did nothing really special. We all had to work that night at Ruby Tuesday, so we planned a party at one of our co-workers house that night to bring in the new year. Drunk a little. Partied. Laughed. Then it was time to go home. Nothing spectacular. Just simple.

Then trouble started. The next month, a week before Valentine's Day, he dumped me! Terrance came to me and said, "I can't do this no more" and gave a big explanation after work one day about how it was rumored I slept with Jabari, this guy that used to work with us. I didn't know where it came from or why. So he told me this, and walked away and out of my life.

During this time, I really panicked and went through a depression. By this time, everyone at work knew we were together, so it was extra uncomfortable when Terrance and I broke up. I wasn't getting any sleep and lost about 10 pounds from not eating. Hair was shedding bad. I was superstressed. Why you ask? *Because of the dumb breakup line, which wasn't at all true.* It was no explanation, just the excuse he wanted to give. So I had to stick with the program and move on.

A month later, at a house warming party for one of our co-workers, Terrance decided to come as well. When he stepped in the house, my co-worker said "Girl, don't even pay him no attention." I didn't trust her too much, because Terrance said she tried to get with him one time, but I did ignore him the entire night and drank more because I didn't want to care that he was there. I felt good. The party was good. Drinking games were going on, food, music... but 3 am hit, and everyone was leaving to go home. Most of us had to be at work the next morning at 10 and those work hangovers have everyone in a very, very slow and grouchy mood. Then I get a tap on my shoulder, as I'm concentrating on where my car was parked. "Amber," Terrance said.

"What?" I said, not looking back at him.

"Can we talk? Please?"

OK, so it's 3 am, I'm drunk, stumbling, trying to find my keys, and wondering how I am going to get all the way to my side of town. And he wants to talk? Doubt it! "Listen, I have to go to work in the morning, so if you want to talk, you can follow me home." He said he would.

Once we got there, we sat on the couch. I looked at him. He looked at me, with his *I know I was wrong* grin back to me. Then there was that dimple! Goodness, that dimple got me every time.

"I want you to know I am sorry," he said. "I should have not believed Dean when she told me about you and Jabari. She came back and said to me that she didn't actually know y'all slept together, but that is what she heard when he came over to your house that day. He said that to her."

"Terrance, you should have believed me. Now I told you, I didn't sleep with him. He came over that one time and watched one movie with me. Then his friend picked him back up and they left. I can't help if Jabari told Dean we slept together. It's my word against his, and he is passed away now so it's just really my word. I can't believe you believed her and not me!" I started to tear up. "What reason I have to lie to you?"

"You don't have a reason to lie to me. I know you telling the truth. I was just scared because he was dirty, and that would have been nasty of you to sleep with him."

"Exactly Terrance." I just shook my head at him. The room was now spinning since I was sitting still and had too much to drink.

"Can we get back together?" he asked.

I looked in his eyes, and honesty filled them. Regret filled them. Apology filled them. "Yes, we can."

***

The next two months, nothing was better at all: rumors of him cheating on me with the Ruby Tuesday hostess, her coming to me telling me what they did, and when they did it. I was just sick to my stomach. There was even one time where I couldn't get in touch with him from 6 in the evening to 10 the next morning. I was up all night sick with worry about where he was and who he was doing it with. I must have called him 90 times, literally. He also lost his job during this time we were together. So I was basically supporting the relationship by paying for dates we would go on, driving him around, letting him live four or five days out of the week at my apartment. It was still too much with Terrance, and I decided to call it quits on him. I took him home one day and told him I couldn't do it anymore. He asked if I was sure, and I told him I was very sure. But we both agreed that being separate was the best route to take.

For a month after, we still messed around with each other. I was in hopes he would change his mind, tell me he would "do better," and really follow through on that promise with actions, but those words never came from his mouth. So we drifted apart and really left each other alone.

THE LIES
THE DEVIL TOLD

After the relationship I had with Terrance, I was in a very dark place. I didn't know what was my next point in my life, or even if God had a plan for my life in this area. What should I do? *Here I am, 26 years old, and it seems like nothing's out there for me. Should stay single for the rest of my life? Should I just kick it with someone and not attach any feelings? What should I do?*

My life became very confusing. There was even an opportunity to date a guy who was engaged! He was funny, very. Physically attractive, not so much. (Not at all really) But he was a friend of mine from work, who I'd known for two years. At work, we would go about our normal routine; I was a server, he was a cook. (Sounds familiar doesn't it?) But the texts we sent to each other during our shifts were less than innocent. We would agree which evenings we would come and visit me. He would come over, drink, chill watch TV. Then he would leave and go home to his fiancé. Did I feel bad? Not at all. Not one bit. I didn't care who he was with, because it isn't like I was doing the cheating, he was. He was coming to me and enjoying my company. That was on him. And I thought I could live this lifestyle. Apparently I wasn't getting married, so this was the next best thing is to just keep company with a man who was already taken. (Sounds like a Lifetime Movie Network movie right?) But I thought, *Yes, I can do "me" and just have artificial insemination from some random guy.* I don't need a baby's father in the life of my child. It'll just be me, my child, and my success. Nothing else. God doesn't have anyone for me. God didn't have that in his plans for me. I'm convinced.

And I was very convinced. I wouldn't, in my sound mind, ever think to look at someone else's man in that type of way, let alone a fiancé. But

I did, and although that period lasted but a very short time, it was still a period where I knew God's plan for my life wasn't working because I was ending in dead end relationships without commitment. Guys didn't want to be with me for me; they were with me because of what I could give them. I was cute, yeah, but I felt like what I was bringing to the table wasn't keeping them interested. So my next best thing to do was to just do to guys what guys do to girls all the time, and that is to play with them, to go into a fling with no real intentions.

The devil told me these lies. He said *God doesn't have a plan for you. You are not on His mind. You will forever be alone. No one will love you. All guys are the same. Might as well do to them what they do to you. Might as well play with them.* And I listened. I gave the devil my ear. I listened and believe that no dude would actually wife me. No man will ever give me his time for real.

But somehow God didn't give up on me – even when I gave up on Him. He swept me right on back, using the hurt to get to healing.

COMING TO CHRIST

That summer, I left for New York City to travel with a group I managed for their annual conference they booked with my company every year. Right before the trip, I trimmed my hair in a short bob style, *no room to make a ponytail* short. I needed to do something drastic. Something that I could remind myself every day, *this is a fresh start.* And still, I was communicating with Terrance throughout the trip. That is because the night before I left for New York, Terrance and I hooked back up. And shortly after my trip, the communication ceased. I was just unhappy with life. I was unhappy with myself. I was tired. I was beat up. I was worn out. I felt used up. I was on empty. I was on zero. And I told myself, *I can't hold on to a false hope that Terrance will eventually come to his senses.* Because he didn't.

So the Sunday following my decision to cut off Terrance communication, I went to church.

My youth pastor and old Sunday school teacher from my church I grew up in had started his ministry less than a year before. My mom tried to get me to go with her a couple of times, but I was busy with work. But not that Sunday. Even though I wasn't accustomed to waking up before 10 on a Sunday, that faint voice from God told me to go. So I finally got up, dressed and went inside the church suite for a word I definitely needed from God.

I don't remember verbatim that Sunday's message, but it captured me, had me wanting to keep coming back for more. And, of the first services I attended, the pastor spoke to me about my past.

From God, he prophesied, *From your past relationships, it has taught you what you needed to look out for in men. Much like the "game" you need to look out for from men. God said "I am teaching you."* Very true. I realized I was dating the same type of men, over and over again, expecting something different. Trying to save a man *who doesn't want to be saved* is as stupid as pulling a stubborn horse to water who's not thirsty. The men I was dealing with were not thirsty. They weren't thirsty for me anyway. They just wanted some company. The thought of having me, or a girl, was nice. But didn't want it for the longevity I was looking for. I wasn't that girl that made them want to settle down. I wasn't that woman that made them want to be faithful to one woman. I wasn't her. And as much as it took for me to swallow that hard pill, I had to do it. I just wanted to be loved.

I didn't want to be on empty anymore, I needed to be filled. I told God, *Look, I'm going to follow you wholeheartedly, like for real. I want to do this thing for real with you.* And that is the moment God led me to be restored and to grow.

God worked in me like only He could. It was a slow process but well worth it! He didn't heal just the heartbrokenness but healed each and every area of my life. That's how God works. Complete surrender is giving up all of your life, to trade it in for His. That's how the church I attended worked. We sometimes want to give God only the area we want Him to fix, but God doesn't want to work that way. To be honest, He can't work that way because the areas of our lives are intertwined and healing as a whole has to take place for complete restoration.

During this time, God spoke to my heart to let go and not date any man that reminded me of the jokers I had dated in my past. So my blinders were completely destroyed, and God caused me to see instantly who were the wolves in sheep's clothing. Sometimes within two minutes of speaking to a guy, I could tell instantly what he was about. Also during this time, He broke off a lot of friendships that weren't good for me. This was hard for me because I thought I could trust the girls who were in my circle, but God revealed to me who wasn't really a friend to me. I cried at those, but there were also some who stayed with me and by my side.

Also during this time, He sanctified my heart. The yearning to commune with God became louder and louder in my spirit, and I built a very tight bond with my church family. The church was small, very small. Maybe 10 members including the Pastor and his wife, but the size didn't matter to me. The approach did. The love for God they showed I never experienced before, and it was so beautiful! It wasn't about the religious acts, it was about adorning God, the keeper of our souls. The church family was humble, approachable and loving – and loved you for where you are and where you were headed.

To this day, that is still my church home. Since the first day I stepped foot in the sanctuary, I've attended every Sunday I could and every Thursday night for Bible expedition. I kept myself in the Word of God and He kept delivering me from what was needed out of my life. Not instantly – but gradually – there were changes the people around me saw, and most importantly, I saw. He worked bit by bit, and is still working 'til this day, so I can be all that He promised I would and I can be

His masterpiece.

HE CAME BACK!

Yes they did…They all did. Each one of them came back to me. But, of course, I wasn't interested anymore in any type of man that wasn't trying to better himself in Christ. I felt I couldn't just revert back to the woman of the world I once was. I had a contract to uphold with God.

About a couple of months after I went back to church, I went to my college homecoming. Every year I would see Camron there at the all black party he threw on campus. And every year he would want some alone time with me to check up on me and to see how I was doing. This year was no different. After seeing him at the all black party, he told me to wait by the bar, as he was going to buy me my drinks for the night. So I waited and told my girls I would catch up with them later. He came moments later, saying how beautiful I was that night and how much he missed me, telling me how dumb he was for mistreating me and letting me go. He wanted me to give him another chance to prove he was not the same guy. He asked me if I could catch up with him after the party. So I obliged and told him I would meet at his hotel.

After the party was over around 2 or so, I told Camron I was going to go ahead to my hotel and he could call me when he was at his hotel. Another hour passed before I got a phone call from him. Inside of me, I was really hoping I wouldn't hear from him. I was hoping he ran into another ex or someone else and forgot all about me. But I got the text *you can come now*. So I drove my car about four blocks from my hotel to his. I gave the bellman my keys, as I entered into the lobby, where he was waiting for me. We went up to his room. There, he had to shower and get undressed, and in the room I waited. He came out in his paid pajama pants and his white tee, and sat on the bed next to me. I felt really uncomfortable! I ninety percent knew where this was leading, but I didn't want to assume.

"You wanted to talk right?" I asked Camron, backing a little ways away from him.

"Yeah, Nikki. I still love you."

I rolled my eyes. "Ok, so what's new? You say this every year, then I don't hear from you until the next year."

"I just be so busy! I get my numbers changed, flights everywhere. But I am real about you." I knew that look he was giving, and I no longer believed it. He was lying. "You can't say you don't love me, right?"

"I can say that, Camron. I am not in love with you anymore. I accept your apology about a lot of things, but you really did me dirty, Camron. And I probably could never trust you." His face sank really low as though the words cut him. "And to be honest, I don't know why I'm here. I'm going to leave."

"No, no, no, you don't have to leave! You can stay here with me. We don't have to do anything. We can just sleep together. I just want to be next to you."

Ok, I thought. Quite frankly, I was really tired and didn't feel like driving back those four blocks back to the hotel. I pushed myself back to head of the bed, and began to get under the covers. He crawled in next to me and turned off the light.

"I love you Nikki," he said getting closer to me in the bed. I kept silent because I didn't want to repeat the words back to him so he could feel better about himself. I was really over him. I was over it. And I didn't want to be in the bed any longer.

I got out of bed and put back on my slippers and hoodie. "Camron, I'm about to leave. I just don't feel right. I don't even know why I came. It's not the same. I don't have feelings for you anymore."

"Don't go. We can just go to sleep." Camron was now pleading. Something I wanted to hear from a man – to tell me not to go – but that didn't even satisfy me. I was numb to him, and I wouldn't have been able to sleep if I stayed. He tried to block my exit out of the room a couple of times before he got the point. He no longer persisted and I was free to go.

"Bye Camron," I said closing the door behind me. I hurried down the hall and to the elevator before he was able to pull a dramatic move behind me. I exited quickly and rang for the bellman to get my car. He looked at me like *Dang, that fast?* I ignored the urge to explain myself, gave him a couple of bucks, and made my way to my hotel.

***

Within a few months, I heard from Charles and Terrance. *What a surprise, right?*

I met up with Charles one day after his text to me saying he wanted to see how I was doing. So I told him I would be over to his house later, once he arrived home and showered and everything. When I was over there, it was like old times again. He seemed really happy to see me and he cooked me some of his "renowned chili" for me. After we ate, we went back to his studio movie room to watch a movie. But before we did we talked.

He looked at me with the most seriousness a man has ever looked at me before. "As a man, Ruby, I want to let you know straight up you are a good girl. Man, I got into the relationship with Trina, and boy was she lazy! I mean, lazy! And I look at you, and I thought about you and I was like *that girl only wanted to be with me.* You cooked. You had a man feeling good. You dope. And all I was going after was her thickness. She had a booty." He laughed. "But that girl gone. And she crazy! You know I moved her in right?"

"What?" I was surprised Charles said he moved a girl into his house.

"Yeah, I moved her in. She would not even clean. Some days, she would be laying in the same spot I left her in. Didn't get up to cook nothing. Man." He started shaking his head. "You are a good one, Ruby, and I mean that from the bottom of my heart. She met my mom, and my mom said *nuh uh!* And she talks about you, seeing how you doing."

Charles was not a man to say sentimental things. I had to learn his language of "sentiment." He never once uttered how much I meant to him, I just assumed by his "doing things" for me was how much he appreciated me. I was in disbelief at this point.

"You know if I we would have still been together, no lie, we probably would have had our kid by now. I messed that up." Charles still had his stern look on his face, but his eyes truly meant he was sorry, and this was his way of apologizing. I just stared back at him.

I would have liked to cry at that moment, but I smiled and said, "Thank you for being real with me."

We continued talk for a while and then watched a movie. I'm glad he realized my worth. But it was just too late for him and I. I had no intention on getting back with him because my commitment to Christ. He would have surely made me fall back into the old ways.

Later that year, Terrance as well decided to call me out of the blue one afternoon after work.

"Hey there," he said on the phone.

"Well hey Terrance. How are you?" I responded nonchalantly. I really didn't want to hear what he had to say. I moved on from him, and gotten into another relationship at this point. Made me hurry him so he could get to his point fast.

"I'm good. What you been up to?" he asked.

I told him about work, still traveling, my upcoming travel plans, and the fact that I was meeting up with my boyfriend later that evening.

"Oh, so how's that going?" he asked.

"Extremely well, Terrance." I laughed.

"Well good. He should treat you good." He started off. His voice then got very serious. "Yeah because I didn't. You were a good girl, Amber. And I was out trying to still do my thing and be with you, and you didn't deserve that. I was good with you. These girls out here, man." He paused. Last time I heard from him he was living with this woman on the northside of town. Probably like a couple of months after we broke up. He was complaining to me about her then, too. I assumed things were still not going well. "Yeah, man. These girls ain't nothing out here. They triflin'. But you was the only girl I had that wasn't playing games with me. So sorry the way things ended and how they did."

"You are good, Terrance. Look, I'm over it. We both moved on. It is what it is at the end of the day." My phone then notified me of an incoming call. "Look Terrance, this is him. I got to go."

"Yeah, ok. Just make sure he treat you right."

"Yeah, he really does. Look, I'll just talk to you later. Take care of yourself. Bye." I hung up with Terrance for John to talk about our plans for the evening.

JOHN

After my dedication to the Lord, and when I decided to fully follow Christ, I was single for a good six months. Through the power of social media, and reconnecting people from our past, I got back in touch with John from high school. I thought he was really cute in high school, but we just became good friends. We had some classes together, and we clowned for the majority of the time. He was goofy, I loved to laugh. We had chemistry, even though I had a boyfriend and he had a girlfriend.

So social media got us back together. I believe he randomly hit me up to see how I was doing, so we chatted for a bit. I told him I was an event coordinator, and that I traveled. He told me he lived for the Lord and was singing for God now. He asked me if I could help him put his album release party together that will be within the next three or four months. I was very happy to do it! It would be one of my first projects with my personal event planning company. So I took on the task. And in the time we were talking on the phone and spending together, we automatically clicked back to that chemistry we had in high school. He was still goofy, and I still loved to laugh. The more and more we conversed, the more and more we started talking about things besides his music…sports, food, cars, clothes, people! We reminisced about high school and talked about our aspirations. Then it clicked to me, *Hey, we're kind of getting close.*

One Sunday afternoon, we were talking on the phone, he surprised me by saying, "Can I be your Valentine?"

I was totally thrown off guard. It was the end of December, I wasn't thinking about Valentine's Day! My history of Valentine's Day really sucked. The best Valentine's Day I had was in the 12th grade when my boyfriend got me balloons, candy, a bear, candles and all that girly stuff. After 12th grade, my Valentine's Day considered of feeling lonely or working. I didn't even count that day as "real." So I smiled at the excitement that someone was thinking of me at least for this Valentine's Day coming up.

"Yeah, you can be my Valentine, John." I smiled and laughed because I felt real silly saying that, almost as nervous he sounded for asking me. We continued our conversation, however in the back of my mind, sparks were flying. *He was interested in me, like for real. A Christian guy I'm feeling I think is feeling me back. Hooray! Amber, you are really changing!* I was really changing. I wasn't interested in the type of guys I used to date. Even going out with friends during my singleness, guys would approach me and off the bat their 'game' disgusted me. I couldn't believe I fell for that, and how silly I was for being giddy about it. Yuck! But this guy, John, was the real deal. He loved the Lord! Yes, I was pretty darn excited!

So within the next couple of weeks, we started being an item. We didn't officially say it, but we were. Talking every day. Seeing each other frequently. The long talks. The laughs. The excitement. Yes, we were a couple. I went and met his family during a family game night they were having. I didn't know I was walking into that. I was just coming to see John. But I pulled up a chair, and played. Nervous as I wanted to be, I tried to relax and be myself around him, his big sister, his mom and dad, and two adorable nephews. But toward the end of the night, everyone was comfortable, and they seemed to like me.

***

Valentine's Day was two weeks away. I didn't know what to expect, but I know he told me it was going to be nice. So I bought a blue peplum classic dress to wear on this special occasion. He said he liked the color blue. So blue was what I planned on wearing that night. I was going to try a simple bun on the top of my head, my hoop earrings, and my leopard wedges heels, topping it off with some red lip stick. I couldn't wait for the day! He sounded excited as I was, especially since he knew that this day was not so special to me. But he wanted to make it, just for me.

The day before Valentine's Day, John called me very stressed and panicked.

"Ok, Ok, slow down, what's wrong?" I said. I wasn't feeling too good that day. Running a fever, so I was laying down in my bed when he called me. "John, what's wrong?"

"So, I call the Sundial today to reconfirm the reservation and to also see if I could bring some flowers before so they could be ready at your table. So why they said they don't have my reservation and they are all booked for Valentine's Day." My heart literally sunk to the bottom of my stomach. I was thinking *what in the world you mean they don't have your reservation?* He continued, "See with them you had to put a card to hold a reservation, and the girl who took my reservation didn't ask for my card, she just put my name and party of two. So after speaking with the girl on the phone I then asked to speak with the manager, and he told me the same thing and that he was sorry and we could go for next week." *Next week! Oh my goodness, next week?* I tried not to panic and to be understanding. He then got quiet on the phone, I guess expecting me to say something back to him.

"Wow John. It's Ok." Disappointed? Yes, I was but disappointments happen. I couldn't pretend they didn't. I couldn't fault him for a mistake the Sundial made. I felt really bad about the situation and I know he felt bad too. But I was saddened. After asking him some more questions about the plans we got off the phone with each other. The news broke me. *Yet, another V-day bites the dust…*I thought. I continue to lay in the bed, my dog was laying with me at the foot of the bed. Thoughts began to wonder…would we go somewhere else? Did he have a backup plan? What was I going to do the next day? Only time would tell, and within a day it did.

The next day, Valentine's Day, we hardly spoke. He called that morning after to talk but sounded so depressed over the phone. I don't even remember what we talked about, but it wasn't about Valentine's Day for sure. So that day was rather lonely for me because I didn't get to see my boyfriend at all, let alone spend time with him. I would have thought at least he would have suggested to see me or something, but there was nothing.

Three days after Valentine's Day, we agreed to go to a local steakhouse. We took our own cars and had a very silent dinner. I felt I was forcing myself to be there, forcing myself to talk. I don't believe I ate all of what I ordered. I just wanted to hurry through dinner and hurry back home. Maybe because Valentine's Day was still bothering me... or the fact he gave me two cookies and crème Hershey Bars and a ginger ale to me right before we walked in. Or maybe the fact I hand crafted a basket full of the things he liked as a present to him only to see there was no "thought" returned to me. Maybe it was the fact this added to the list of bad Valentine's Day in my book. Maybe. But I know that I wasn't *feeling* the gesture to me that day. Not after almost two months he excited me about it.

But I got over it.

The next months were fine. Even though we didn't go out that much, we spent time either at his home or my house. He would cook, and invite me over. I would cook, and invite him over. Watch TV. Cuddle. Talk about our lives. We were comfortable and moved forward from that Valentine's incident.

March of that year, I thought of a really good idea to go to Nashville together. (Anyone who knows me, knows I love the city of Nashville.) I believe I was telling him about the hotel Gaylord Opryland Resort, and it sparked his interest as well. I told him of all the connections I have in Nashville as far as the hotel, the touring and everything. He told me "Let's go then." And I got really excited! I would take care of everything, and we agreed he would take care of the rental car. He said that was cool, and he would get that situated. And there it was, our first trip!

Leading up to the July Fourth weekend, the weekend we agreed to go to Nashville, we had a few dates, and I went to a few performances he was invited to minister to. He went to a couple of my church services, but for the most part, we chilled at my house. Since he lived with his mom, I believed he found it more comfortable to come to my house most of the time. He came over and fixed some things, and promised to fix others. He even took me to the airport when I had to travel to Las Vegas for my job, and came to pick me back up to take me back home.

The week of the Nashville trip, I was going over everything I had booked with him, and what we were going to do when we get there. I couldn't wait to see Nashville on the Fourth of July, at night was going to be a city wide fireworks explosion that I couldn't wait to see and share the experience with him. He said he was going to get the rental on the day before, so everything was a go.

Or so I thought.

"Yeah, so I went up there because the guy I talked to this morning said he was going to hold the car. And when I got there, it was already off the lot!" John said on the phone the day before we were supposed to leave.

"So?" I questioned to him, replaying the Valentine's Day in my head. "There wasn't another car? Did you put down your card before you went up there? They can't give your car away you reserved."

"Well the other truck, it was going to be more than what I planned on. I didn't put the card on because he told me he would hold it for me. So now I am trying to ask my dad if we can use the truck. But he isn't sure about it yet."

I wanted to scream! This was a definite replay, and I was furious. "So, are you saying we are going or not? I have to cancel this reservation today because if I don't, I'll be charged for one night."

"I don't know yet. Let me call you back."

It was around six in the evening. I was trying to stay calm as I could, but already thinking I know what this outcome will be. By eight that night, I texted him I was cancelling the hotel reservations. I couldn't afford to pay for a hotel night I will not be staying in. Then I texted my sister and told her I would be going with her out of town with family for my July Fourth plans. Done.

The next morning, as I was getting ready to meet at my sister's house, I get a call from John.

"Hey, so are we going or not?" he asked.

"What do you mean? Did you get my text last night? I canceled the room."

"Oh." He paused for a minute. "Ok."

"Ok." I ended the call and continued to get ready to meet my sister. That day I thought, *I didn't have time for that.*

***

As that week was ruined for our six-month anniversary, he did bring me a gift until the next week. As he walked in the door with flowers, a teddy bear, a card, a tote bag and Beyoncé Heat perfume, of course I was quick to forgive him. He apologized again about the previous week, and I believed him. He wrote a little personal note in the card:

Happy Anniversary to my friend, my girl, my future wife, my business partner, future mother of my kids. You've made me the happiest man on earth. I love you! Look forward to many more & an amazing life with you! Love you, John

We began to move forward, continuing to see each other and continued in the relationship. He had to swallow a hard pill when he learned I would be unavailable for a few days because of my church cruise to the Bahamas. He continued to tell me he would be lonely without me, but he promised he would be focused hard on his music while I was gone. And yes, those days flew by, and I missed him very much. I couldn't wait to get back to him.

When we arrived back in Port Canaveral after our cruise, some drama with some of the cruise participants had everyone in a sour mood on the seven-hour ride back to Atlanta. During this time, I kept texting John on my phone about all that happened and how I was unhappy and frustrated. He kept me calm, almost getting frustrated himself I was so upset. As soon as I got back, he met me back at my house to tell him all about the trip.

However, after mid August, things were a little bit different for me in regards to John. I started to get unhappy. As much as he kept telling me about *how many people are using him for his studio services and not paying him*, he remained at their disposal. I kept trying to give him advice, but it started to get repetitive. We weren't going out anymore, if we ever did. In the eight months of being together, I could count the times on my hand we actually went out on a date. We were always at my house or at his house. In the back of my mind, I kept questioning him about everything. I lost my trust in him. The two major things we planned failed, and I didn't want to be hurt or disappointed again. I didn't want to be lied to. Every day I lost more and more emotion for him. As much as he tried to tell his "woe is me" stories, I had enough. I wanted him to own up to the things, but not make excuses for them. I felt like he wasn't making moves anymore and I felt like he had given up.

I knew our relationship was ending when our conversations were short and lifeless. We finally went on date, our last one, to another steakhouse. For the entire meal, we didn't say one word to each other. Not one. We told the waiter our order and sat in silence. Through the waiting for the meal. Through the meal. Through getting the check. No words. When he returned me back to my house, he didn't want to leave that way. He wanted to talk. And we did. But I just couldn't be with him anymore. I would always wonder *what's next* with him. I could tell it wasn't what he wanted to hear, but he understood, went to his car and left.

Within the next couple of days, we met up to exchange some things we had from each other. That moment was the last time I saw or ever spoke to John.

SOMETIMES IT'S JUST
A FLING

Flings are what they are. I don't consider anything less than two months worthy of putting myself in a relationship category with any guy, even if I am exclusive with them.

But there were some flings after my relationship with John, talking here and there, but it was nothing serious. I would entertain guys for the fun of it, because surely as I was certain, John and I would eventually get back together. Even though I felt I made the right decision in breaking up with him, I knew there was a chance to rekindle and work back.

So I continued to live my life. Men were approaching me left and right, exes were still trying to come back in the picture, but I just didn't want any ol' guy. I wanted him. My husband. The one God promised to me. The one who God said was on his way to me. I wanted it to be him next, not another failed relationship.

There was a guy who started chatting with me through social media: Derik. The backstory on him...Derik's friend, Chris started as the sound engineer at my church a couple of months prior to breaking up with John. So I believe Chris told Derek about me since he noticed I was a single woman and Derik was his single friend. Derik friended me on social media but didn't start to communicate until a few weeks after that. After I accepted his friend request, I was seemingly interested in him. He was very handsome, a musician with a great indie soul voice, and seemed like he kept fit athletically. Plus, he seemed to be a romantic, much like who I thought I was. But to be honest, from first glance, I thought he was some sort of local big shot musician to even want to be with someone like me. I was very shocked when he did finally reach out, but reluctant as well to continue to talk to him.

Our first conversations on the phone were very sweet. The "getting to know" you stages are pretty much like that anyway. The "Oh, how nice!" and "Oh, me too!" giggles and laughs we had among the many conversations we first had over the phone. He seemed pretty nice and laid back, so my attention was focused on him for the time, and I wasn't interested in talking to anyone else.

Our first date was at the big park in downtown Atlanta. Somewhere I never been as a date, but only dreamed about going one day. You know *holding hands in the park, grabbing some ice cream, strolling along having conversation?* So I was excited about going, because this told me a lot about him.

"Hello? I'm here by the Ferris wheel, where are you?" I asked Derik, on my cell phone approaching the park around two that nice October afternoon.

"Hey, I'm here too," Derik said. "I'm coming toward the wheel now." I heard him on the phone taking his strides. And as I was still walking toward the gate, I see a nice looking guy across the street on the phone waving at me. "Hey, is that you in the pink shirt?" he asked.

I laughed. "Yes, that's me. I see you." I walked fast across the road before the traffic came. Derik was still walking toward me, as we met in the middle on the sidewalk. We greeted each other with a hug. And as we both walked toward the entrance of the park, I was taking my "too little steps," as he was taking his strides toward an empty park bench. It was crowded that Saturday.

We talked for hours, and I mean hours. We laughed, joked and conversed for nearly four hours or more. Because by the time we walked toward our cars, the sun already had set. The time flew by, as we told each other about ourselves, plans, dreams, fears and ambitions. Very much like a scene from a movie to me, I was very satisfied with our first date at the park. The night ended with a kiss from him, which he told me "felt like the perfect opportunity against the backdrop of the Atlanta skyline." Indeed, that was a very romantic move he made, however, I didn't know how I felt about it.

From then on, we conversed through the phone, and went on several dates. I was very intrigued about him, what he did musically and his goals in life. In the back of my mind, I was preparing as if I was going to be his wife one day. *I mean, what about the spotlight? What about this? How good of a wife would I be? Is he my husband, God?* Those thoughts were floating around in my head, seriously. What if he was the one? But I didn't want to start off too fast with these thoughts, as they tend to rush in my mind prematurely, I didn't want to get excited over something I didn't know about for sure.

One day at a restaurant, Derik caught me off guard. "You never offer me anything off your plate when we go out to eat," he said.

I looked clearly stunned at his question to me, looking like he was very serious about it. I really didn't know what to say so my reply was, "Did you want something off my plate?"

"Oh, no, you're good. I'm just saying," he said, in his nonchalant demeanor he sometimes had. Even though he said it was "no biggie," I could tell it sort of was a big deal. The rest of the night to me, felt a little awkward because I didn't know what to do at that point. I was cautious, and made aware, that's what he liked, for his woman to offer her food to him. Like in an earlier instance he told me not to call him "shawty" because that signified us being "friends" and not more than friends. The term *shawty* was Atlanta jargon I used every so often, probably since I was sixteen. I used it here and there in place of someone's name. Instead of calling him Derik, when I would jokingly call him *shawty*.

From then, I was a little apprehensive. *What to and what not to do? What to and what not to say?* It was sort of like trying to read his mind and trying to do things for him I thought he would want me to do. So I was very conscious of what I did from then on out, being mindful of everything. And this is when I started to get in an uncomfortable place. But in an effort to keep him from trying to walk away, I did the very best I could to keep him well and pleased.

We were intimate a few times. This was something I knew better than doing, especially in writing a blog entitled "My Oath to Celibacy" and liturgical dancing for my church. And in times where temptation got strong, I wasn't strong enough to hold back my desire, and Derik wasn't as prudent with it either. Every time we had sex, I literally cried with so much sadness that I couldn't keep my vow to God. Every time I told Him "no more," and every time I failed Him. I desperately was trying to establish boundaries with Derik, who was intrigued at the idea, but never really pulled through during the moment. I felt awful.

So all of this was going on in my mind, and I didn't know how to address Derik about it. (Not to mention the fact he had a really close relationship with a female friend as well.) I didn't think Derik was the one, and I didn't think we should continue with whatever we were doing. But I didn't want to be the person who gave up either. These weren't deal breakers for me. I felt we could develop discipline. I could help him understand why I felt his relationship with his female friend was rather close. I also prayed he would understand why I walked on eggshells around him.

But Derik was the one that broke it to me that "maybe we are not compatible" conversation to me. (It's amazing how God will end a relationship when you won't.) He questioned whether I was happy because I didn't seem like I was. He said I started to complain about little things and he didn't like that I didn't too much care for his relationship with his female friend. He also said I wasn't supportive of him and his career. Of course, I was devastated and confused because I felt him walking out of the relationship. I really just wanted to be with him and make things work. I wanted him to understand that relationships are about give and take, and sorting out the issues instead of walking away from them altogether. But that was what he wanted to do. That was what he felt like he needed to do. So we ended it.

CAGE

"Hey, so just checking on you. How are you doing?" I messaged him on social media. Cage actually first messaged me very shortly after I began entertaining Derik. I wasn't ready to go into anything then, so I quickly responded to Cage's first message with "I am involved." He respectfully went away after that, but we remained friends on the Internet.

But this time I wanted him to know I was not involved anymore. Why? Because, I was very interested in him! I wanted man of God. Someone who personally knew God, had a relationship with Him, and someone I knew that was going to protect my purity, and mean it. (This was very important to me.) When he first friended me on social media, I checked him out, and he seemed very well into ministry and I could tell he loved the Lord. He wasn't bad looking either! He was also friends with some mutual friends of mines who are on fire for Christ. So sure, why not?

"Hey Amber, how are you?" he finally responded to me.

"Oh, I am well, thanks for asking. I was just checking on you, seeing how you were doing since the last time we talked?"

"Oh, yes, everything has been good with me!" he responded. We chatted briefly online, and he finally asked, "So are you still involved? I just don't want to be disrespectful?"

"Well, no. I was more emotionally involved than anything when I first messaged you. I still needed to recoup from the last relationship I was in."

"I understand that."

"Ok, well, you take it easy Cage. Nice speaking with you."

"Well is it ok to have your number and call you sometime?" he asked.

Yes! He was respectful! He didn't say *let me have your number*. He didn't give me his number. He asked me. "Sure. It is…" I gave him my number and we ended our online conversation.

About two weeks later he called me. I totally forgot about giving him my number, and we didn't speak no more through social media. I was at home frying fish one evening after work and heard my cell phone ring. Looking down at my cellphone, and the unknown number was about to go to voicemail when I remembered *Cage*. I answered. We spoke no longer than thirty minutes before he had to get off the phone and do some other things. However from first talk, I had butterflies. I really hoped that I made a good impression on him, being that he was more seasoned as a Christian than I was, so I hope I didn't have too much "world" in me for him to scare him away.

We continued to talk that week before our first date the next week. He came to my house, with some white roses, and escorted me to a contemporary upscale restaurant in Atlanta. I've been there before for a group I managed, but not to dine, so this would be a first experience for me. The atmosphere was very nice for the two of us to talk, and we managed to get through the meal without any awkward silent moments, which was great. He got to know more about me, I got to know more about him. Everything was good for the first date, as well as on the ride home. When we arrived back at my house, we sat in the car for a minute and talked some more. I knew I should've just said "goodnight" to him and went inside the house, even though I didn't want to; I didn't want him to seem like I was eager. But we sat and continued in conversation, and he suddenly leaned over and kissed me. I was shocked, as I thought to myself, *am I that girl that gets kissed every first date?* I laughed, he smiled. We ended the evening, and I wished him a safe drive back.

From that day on, I woke up with butterflies every morning from him. Cage and I just clicked, I felt that we did anyway. The "good morning" texts started. The daily conversations started. Our thing kind of took off, even though it wasn't "official." I was not seeing or entertaining anyone else so he had all of my attention. From the looks of it, I had his as well. With the following months, we did some really cool things like go to a Christian comedy show and shoot at the gun range. We had dinner and movie dates. He came to see me dance liturgically within a month of us meeting! I grew super excited about him. I could tell he did too after he invited me to come to his baby brother's baby shower, where his mom would also be in attendance. I was nervous, to say the least, but she was very inviting to me when she saw me. I could tell good things were said about me to her. (Sometimes I asked Cage what he said about me to her, and he wouldn't tell me.) But I knew he was all about me when he sent a one-month anniversary picture to my phone one day while I was out of state.

"Happy 1 month anniversary," it read, "I hope you are doing good up there!" I was in the middle of another chaotic scene with one of my travel groups in Minneapolis. The group size increased to the point there was no food for the additional people. The client was getting upset with me, asking me "How could this happen?" and I was running around frantic trying to find food for the group. But when I reached for my phone and read the text from Cage, I grew really calm. (I called him back later after my event and we chatted that evening until I was tired.)

To me, everything was happening so fast with Cage, but the feelings were indeed mutual. It got to a point where he had put my picture on his social media page as his "Woman Crush Wednesday". (That was a trend on social media where people would post their women crushes, their wife, girlfriends or sometimes celebrities.) His dedication to me was powered by his amazement of who I was. I felt I was put on a very high pedestal, and his thoughts toward me were amazing. I was also a little skeptic about it, because we were literally a little over a month into our relationship, but it seemed it came from a very honest pace. I returned my feelings about him to my social media world two or three weeks after that, showing off how great and endearing of a guy he was. I went to his church and attended Bible study and met his pastor, and he came to mine as well. Normally I am a little apprehensive about attending a church service with a guy I was interested in because his worship may not have been the same type as mines, but I didn't feel that way with him. We were even praying together at nights before bed.

So we grew, but definitely had some minor hiccups in the road, even right before we were going in a Christian café on a Friday night. Something about me he didn't like: I shut down and fake a smile when I don't feel like I can't get my point across to the other person. We had one of those disagreements where he thought one way, and I was on another page about a particular subject. I felt talking to him about the problem made it worse because I felt like it wasn't saturating in his mind my point of view. But he turned the flame down on our argument that night, and we continued to enjoy the spoken word, live music and band at the Christian café. Another night as we sat in the car in front of his apartment, I lost my cool and yelled at him in frustration. That particular night he was telling me of the "attitude issues" I had and that I needed to work on them. I told him the attitude I probably have comes from being raised in a home of four girls and a mother. And I screamed at him, something along the lines of *that's all I grew up around!*

"You need to watch how you say things, because I don't do yelling. As you see, I am calm and I want that in return," Cage told me.

"But you are not getting what I'm saying! I can't change overnight!" Tears started to swell up in my eyes because of the frustration. "You want me to do that." I was a person who took criticism. When someone tells me something about myself, I really try to change it, especially if it goes against the Fruits of the Spirit. So when he told me about my attitude, I was willing to change it, but I just didn't know how.

"That is not what I want you to do," he said.

"It seems like it," I responded. We calmed ourselves as we continued to talk for another 20 minutes. We wished each other a good night, and I text him when I got back to my place, which was about 15 minutes later. After that night, I realized I was in one of those *outside myself* moments. Anger and frustration took over me. I hated that we didn't see eye to eye, as well as our communication issues. If we could get through that, we would be ok.

What I didn't too much care for was that Cage referenced his last "real" relationship many times. He brought up her name, her daughter, and what she did to him too many times for my liking. When she came to his church, he just had to mention it to me. When she called him by mistake one time, he mentioned it to me. Even when we were at an amusement park with our married friends, and he referenced her again! With how the context of the conversation was going, I was so upset he *mentioned her and not me.* I would have thought they were still in a relationship if I didn't know better! But mostly, he said he mentioned her because he vowed to himself that he would not get into another argumentative relationship. He referenced back to her when one of our conversations grew to a disagreement or argument. I tried so hard not to be "that" person. Of course, I wanted to be the "good thing" he said I was. But I didn't want to have to keep proving myself because of what his ex had done to him. I was beginning to feel I needed to be careful about what I said or didn't say, and also to hold my tongue about the things that bothered me.

But our relationship continued gracefully, as we spent more and more time with each other. After every disagreement, we found our way back to a place of loving each other. Yes, love. We definitely loved and cared for each other tremendously. He slipped those three letter words out first by mistake, which my heart melted! He said I love you around the time I lost my purity ring. Then he gave me a promise ring – not so much to promise to be with me, but to promise to keep ourselves pure before marriage, and to protect that oath I vowed to God for purity. We were obviously inseparable and very much involved relationally on social media as well. All the guys that followed me knew I had a man, and all the girls knew Cage had a woman.

His birthday came, and I wanted to gather his friends and family to join him in go cart racing and a dinner in honor of him. I made it affordable to where everyone paid half of their admission, and I would pay the rest of their admission. I just wanted everyone to be there for him for his birthday and celebrate him. The weekend of his birthday I was in Nashville for a corporate group attending to their events. So right before I left for the weekend, I made him a low country boil, arranged a game and movie night for just the two of us, and also gave him a birthday card. The weekend after I arrived back was the party I threw for him, which everyone enjoyed. My family, his family, and his friends all had a blast.

But the misunderstandings, the small bickering and the famous question "Are you happy?" continued. I got to the point where I thought it would be a good idea to write him an email expressing from my heart. I told him God led me to write the letter to him, since there was a barrier of communication. I wrote about my expectations and concern with the relationship. I told him since he didn't have a car, I expected every now and then to put gas in my car. I told him I didn't like it when he brought up his ex. I told him how I feel misunderstood so many times. I wrote this all in an email to him, along with some other things that were really pressing on my heart and bothering my spirit.

He took the letter as degrading the way I spelled out some stuff to him, especially about the car. He told me, "This letter didn't come from a place of God." He told me that he didn't know if he could ever swing back into the relationship after this, because he didn't feel like a man anymore. Afterwards, he convinced me writing was a bad way to express my feelings, but I told him writing was the only way I could finish my thoughts. To me he always dismissed my ideas or cut me off mid sentence if we had talked. Days after the conversation we had about the letter I wrote, I apologized fervently to him every day within that next week. The last thing I wanted to do was make him feel "less," but my words apparently made him feel that way.

A month or so later, his friend, Ari was in the final stages of prepping to be married in early August that year. He mentioned to her about me earlier in the year I coordinate weddings, and she hired me! (Cage was also in the wedding as a groomsmen, so I was excited to be the overseer of the wedding happenings for her.) Nervous, I was, but I wanted to put on a good impression to Ari. The planning was great, until I received a bad report from Ari on the way I handled the rehearsal, and she didn't feel comfortable about it. She called me that night after the rehearsal and told me, "So, some of the girls said that you had an attitude about the way you handled things tonight." Those words cut very deep. I apologized to her and told her that "when I am hired to do something, I take it very serious. Everyone knows each other, I don't know anyone. I have been told I am very abrupt, but this is business to me." This haunted me the rest of the night, and on into the next day – the day of the wedding. Cage and I rode together, and I told him that morning what Ari told me.

"See, I told you about your attitude," Cage said while driving to the church. "I know how you are, so it rolls off my shoulders from time to time, but they don't know you. You have to be careful, sweetie, because people are not me. You can't be saying 'well this is me' because people don't know you like that."

That day, I felt two blows to my stomach. "But I didn't mean it like that,. I give off that impression when I am working, but I didn't mean it like that."

"I know, but just be careful."

I was very worried about how everything would go. But the Lord smiled on me that day. As much as I was nervous about the girls arriving at the church, they actually warmed up to me a little bit. I tried to keep my words very short to them while still doing my job as the coordinator. Everyone was pleased at the end of the night. I was even proud of Cage that he remained well-mannered and respectful to me, knowing his ex was also in the wedding party. She was even cordial to me. Cage stayed and helped me after everyone was gone so I could finish my job.

By September, I recognized he stopped praying with me at night. I noticed one night we didn't pray after a disagreement we had, in which we normally come together to do. But we continued in the relationship, as I saw nothing that seemed to be alarming we couldn't fight our way through. We invited a close married couple, Devin and Alana, over for a BBQ at my house, as a double date plus to talk about the ins and outs of relationships, man's ways versus woman's ways, and so forth. It was so much insight for me coming from a young couple like them because they had been there, where Cage and I were trying to get on the same page with each other. I felt it really helped us to move forward with each other. Cage and I talked to each other that night, and I told him, "I wish we could talk things out like this all the time. Very calm. I believe we can get somewhere if we could do this often instead of butting heads."

He told me, "You can't do that, Amber. You can't hold a regular conversation."

Cage set up a birthday dinner for me and invited my family and friends to celebrate. The night was awesome. Two days later, we had yet again miscommunication where he thought one way, I thought another way. Which led to days of little to no communication with each other. I didn't know what to do or say at that point to him. I was really trying to refigure how to adjust my life to just make him happy. I even called Alana, and she gave me some words and told me to call his momto get some wisdom

"So, I wasn't going to hear from you today huh?" Cage asked one Thursday night as I was headed to bible study.

"Yeah, I was going to text you," I told him.

"You were going to text me?" He sarcastically laughed in the background. "Well I am calling you to let you know I don't want to pursue the relationship anymore. I lied to you the other day when you asked me was I happy. I said I was and I am not. I haven't been happy in months, and I don't want to pursue this relationship anymore. I think you are delusional, and you need help with that."

That was a soccer punch kick to my stomach, as my heart sank to the bottom and my whole being froze. "Well, Cage. If that is what you want to do, I can't stop you from making up your mind. I don't want that to happen, but if you feel like that's what you have to do." I was hoping he was joking with me.

"Yeah, that's what I want to do." His tone was serious.

"Well ok then."

"OK. Bye."

My throat felt like it closed. I couldn't breathe. I burst into tears still driving headed towards my church.

I had a choice. Do I go, or do I not go to bible study? I was already virtually there, but I didn't want anyone to see me how I was. The red eyes. The bawling and crying. I didn't want the people I worshipped with every Sunday to see me as this total mess. Not Amber. This was not her! As I tried to walk in with my head high, I just couldn't keep my composure that evening. My First Lady called me to the back to talk, and I just bawled into her arms, weak with no strength, no words but "he left me! he left me!"

Such a lady of strength, she showed me what real encouragement was that night! "No, No, don't say that about yourself. You are too good! And if he didn't see it, so be it! You are strong. You will get through this." She had so many words to say to me that night, words I didn't believe. I just keep asking myself, why do bad things happen to good people? I was good to Cage!

But, that was the end. From that day, Cage's voice grew cold to me. His ways toward me were like that of a stranger. As I desperately tried to get him to understand he had already put his foot down. I dropped off some things I had of his and retrieved the things that belonged to me. I called him a couple of times and went over his house once in a desperate attempt to allow him to see my side. I thought when you wanted something so bad, you did what it took to get it. I thought if I showed him I didn't want it to end, that it would soften his heart a little. I never did that to any man. I never begged for anyone back, so I thought this time around I would show that to Cage. But he didn't budge. The pictures of us came off his social media profiles. His calls ceased. The communication ended. Once I saw he was for real, I deleted all memories of him – from the phone, from social media, from the emails. After the last attempt, I collected everything; every card with his love expressed every shirt and even the ring, packed it up nicely in a grocery bag and took it to the donation center box in the supermarket parking lot. As far as I knew, all of what he told me was a lie. The words expressed, the meaning of the ring and the memories, were lies. And the day I took everything out of my house was the last day of holding on. That was really the end.

RECOVERY DONE RIGHT

Ever had someone tell you, "Well just get over it!" And now I laugh, because it's so easy to say. I used to be that person that gave that particular advice. *Girl, get over it! His loss! You too good for him anyway. On to the next one.* We never tell people how to get over it, we just expect people to miraculously shake it off in a day and continue on. We tell people to pile things on top of the hurt so they can get their minds off the pain for a while. But all we are doing is hurting them more, and prolonging their recovery process.

After Cage broke up with me, the wind was knocked out of me for weeks. I could not sleep, I could not eat. For the life of me, I was trying to figure out why, replaying the conversations we had over and over again. Replaying that email I typed to him. Replaying the birthday dinner the week before. Replaying him saying over and over and over again *I want you to be the Mrs. You are my rib. You are my wife. You are my diadem.* Replaying the joyful moments. Replaying the harsh moments. Replaying the moments I could have been better. Replaying the moments I wish he understood. I should have contacted his mother sooner, that maybe, it would have been a different phone call that night. For weeks and months, my mind was on replay and rewind. The *how he could do this to me?* The *I should have known better.* The *Why did I miss the signs?* The *Will he come around?* The *Do he miss me?*

One day I called Alana yet again. I really respect her in so many ways. Not the obvious fact she was a Christian, but she exemplified everything and epitome of Godly wife being so young! We established a friendship from our liturgical dancing, and maintained it through the years. I told her how I was feeling about the entire breakup. I know it was probably hard on her to give advice because she was also friends with Cage, and her husband worked with him. She knew Cage only on the friendship level, so it was probably hard for her to give advice or counsel.

"Girl, you would not believe what I did!" I called her one afternoon. I feared she will judge me, but I didn't know where else to go.

"Girl, what?" she asked.

"So last night, right? I really couldn't sleep! So I woke up at three tossing and turning, this thing been so heavy on my mind. So I get up, put on clothes, and drive over to Cage house."

"Mmm hmm."

"So I get over there, and I am knocking on the door. I am calling him. And he doesn't come to the door, but finally he did. Probably upset I woke him up out of his sleep. He let me in and put on a shirt and stood there before me. So I tell him that I can't sleep or anything. I don't have no one to talk to. I can't understand why he did what he did."

"Mmm hmm."

"Girl, I was looking rough and looked like so desperate, but I really love him."

"So what did he say?"

"I mean, he didn't tell me what I wanted to hear. He told me that he was sorry that I couldn't sleep, but I need to take that up with God. He said I was making the situation an idol. He told me 'seek first the Kingdom of God and his righteousness.' Then he told me there was nothing to be said, that he said all he had to say about it. He doesn't understand why I don't understand the situation. I told him I couldn't get my head around it. I asked him why it took so little for him to leave me. But he had no words. I don't know. I guess I was waiting for him to say something different, or that he changed his mind."

"You know, I knew you was going to say that," she said. "That you got up and went over there in the middle of the night."

"You think I'm crazy, don't you?"

"No, I don't think that. I think you felt like you needed to do that. But girl, you don't need someone like that, who is going to leave you with something so small. You don't want a husband like that. You want someone that will stick with you through thick and thin. Not when it gets hard. I don't know Cage like that, I only know him from hanging around him. But girl, you will be ok. God says everything works for the good of those who love Him and are called according to his purpose for them. And you are called according to His purpose Amber. I don't know. Maybe you can write some scriptures down and put them around your house and keep reciting them. There's something about the Word of God that when you say His promises, it's refreshing. So maybe you can try that?"

"Thanks girl, thank you so much!" It was what I needed to hear that day.

"You're welcome. Let me pray with you real quick." She prayed to God for my strength in this time in my life and to restore me. "I'm going to keep praying for you, girl Love ya."

"Love you too. Take care. Bye!" We hung up.

The incident I told her about happened the night before, so I was really, really mentally and emotionally exhausted. The courage it took to allow Cage see me at an emotionally weak position was huge, but that was the only thing I knew to save what I wanted. The other exes I tooted my nose up and continued on. So if he saw I really cared about him, I really loved him and really wanted to be with him, then I thought he would stay. I started crying out to God after the phone conversation. And after, I opened my Bible app, and the scripture of the day was Jeremiah 29:11: "For I know the plans I have for you, declares the Lord. Plans to prosper you and not harm you, plans to give you hope and a future." I then knew God was tentatively listening to my cry.

The recovery didn't happen overnight. Matter of fact, I felt so attached to Cage, mentally, spiritually and emotionally. And for the life of me, I couldn't figure out why. Normally dealing with a break up, I would have my moment of sadness, almost leading to depression, but this guy stuck around in my head for months. And as hard as I tried not to think about him, as hard as it was to fight the thought of him, I thought about him every day. Some days it angered me, some days I was frustrated, some days I was sad, and some days I was hopeful. But I knew what I had to do. And that was the fight to move from this place.

What this breakup ignited in me was the anointing overflow in my writing. And it may have been the push I needed, but blogs after blogs that flowed out of me for my website, to where I was on a two-month backlog of articles awaiting to be published! I wrote about God's Will. I wrote about loss. I wrote about the broken place. I wrote about the real meaning of love. I wrote about self worth. Topics and subjects were flowing readily out of me. My hands began to type at work sometimes, or through text if I was nowhere near a computer. God let me pour out my hurt through my writing. He didn't allow me to vent out my hurt on social media. He didn't let me vent back to Cage. As much as I wanted to tell him how much I was hurt, God told me to close that door, and don't ever open it again.

I blocked him. Everything about him I blocked. His phone calls. His text messages. His social media for a while. I even blocked some of the mutual friends on social media. I wasn't being childish or malicious, but I did for healing. I knew what I could and could not handle. The possibility of seeing a picture from him, or seeing his name would turn my stomach, and release hurt I was trying to heal. It was something I had to do. It was something that needed to be done to heal. As I was committed to moving on, I had to do this.

God sat me down in this very lonely place where it was me and him. I needed to know what to do at this point. I laid it all out to him:

Lord, I am so tired. I am tired of being hurt. I am so tired of picking and choosing the wrong one. I don't like myself, God. What is it about me that they don't want to stay? What is it about me that they want to leave? Why do they ask me to trust them, and then turn around and still leave? Why can't I keep a man? Why can't I ever do anything right? Why even when I am trying my best, it is not good enough for anyone? Lord, please tell me why you made me like this? Why I have to keep getting hurt? What is it I'm not learning? Oh, Lord, please come to my rescue right now. My heart is broken, it's shattered Lord! It hurts God! I will never be good enough to anyone God! Lord, please take this hurt! Please take away the pain…I can't deal with it. God, if you do this, Lord I'll know it's a miracle.

That is how I felt. It would be a miracle to come out of the lonely, hurting place I was in. I couldn't see a way out, but I prayed to God every day to heal the hurt. And while I was praying to God every day, the Holy Spirit led me to replay the sermons from my pastor and take notes at home so I could really "get it." The Holy Spirit led me to read from other Christian bloggers how to cope with hurt and how to continue after being broken. There was a light - as much as I felt only my world was crashing down, there were others who have been in the same predicament or worse. God led me to a season of just quietness. A season of stillness and growth. Because I was on empty, and there wasn't anyone who could fill me but God. I came home every day and read, prayed and cried out to God. I was still releasing hurt. I was still praying to be whole. For weeks of just nothing but Him and I. Just me and God, gutting out all of the hurt I experienced in all of my relationships. But God also put it on my heart to apologize to John. Yes John. He told me *you know you did the very same thing to John.* And you know what? I did. He could have been trying his best in the relationship, and I was blinded by my own selfishness to not see that. Because I didn't have John's number anymore, I wrote him this social media message:

Hi there! I'm writing you because I wanted to say sorry to you for the way and how things ended. I didn't feel the need until now. As the tables have been turned on me, God really convicted me about doing the same thing to you. So it may not mean anything but just wanted to say "I apologize" and also congrats to you and your fiancé as well! Blessings to you. Bye!

I didn't know what to expect, or even if he would want to forgive me. But I had to be obedient to the Lord. But John did respond and was very nice about it. He thanked me, but he said he really didn't need an apology from me. He also hoped I was doing well and extended prayers to me for what I was going through. My heart was at least happy for that.

God then began to reveal Himself a little bit more to me and the instruction on my life. He told me to meditate on what He said specifically about me. And I began to read the scriptures Philippians 1:6, Psalms 37:23-24, Ephesians 2:10, Psalms 139:10 and Isaiah 43:4. He also assured me John 13:7. Those scriptures went on sticky notes to my bathroom mirror. Also, listening to sermons on the Internet, I specifically wrote down a piece from a Joyce Meyers found on YouTube.

She took out a piece of paper and read from it:

> I know God created me, and I know He loves me
> unconditionally.
> I know I have faults and weaknesses, and yes I want to
> change.
> But I believe God is working in my life, and I believe He's
> changing me day by day.
> While He's doing it, I can still enjoy myself. I can still enjoy
> life and can still be a blessing to other people.
> Although I do have faults, I also have strengths.
> I'm going to maximize my strengths instead of focusing on
> my weaknesses.
> I like myself. I don't like everything I do, and I want to
> change, but I like myself!
> I like what God has created!
> I don't want to ruin the life that Jesus died to give me by
> rejecting myself.
> My worth and value is not based on how other people have
> treated me, or what they thing about me, or what they say
> about me.
> It is based on the fact that God created me, and Jesus died
> to redeem me, and He loves me.
> Therefore I can love myself, and therefore I am able to love
> other people.

And as much as I didn't believe what I was reciting at first, more and more God planted those words in my heart and in my spirit, to where I start believing them. More importantly I started to believe Him. God spoke to my spirit, and let me in on what He thought about me. *Amber, I have placed greatness on the inside of you. I chose you to do this. Just because he didn't see it, doesn't mean that it's not there. KNOW WHAT I SAID ABOUT YOU. If it doesn't agree with what I said, it doesn't matter. You still have a purpose, and My will for your life will still be done. You are still My child. I still have you.*
With this, God started sending people left and right to confirm what

He said about me. My dance instructor assured me *You are so obedient and a child of God. God is pleased with you.* A close and dear pastor pulled me to the side and told me. *I have a ring, and you know it's worth $25,000, but the pawn shop owner is only offering you $25? But you know what the ring is worth. Know your worth. The anointing defends itself, and some people can and some people cannot handle it.* My first lady of my church assured *God is so pleased with you! He knows. He knows your heart.* Even ex-boyfriends and friends came out of nowhere and told me *That man stupid to let you go. There's nobody out there, and no good quality women nowadays. You have a good heart. You were a good girlfriend. You are rare, Amber, and don't you forget that.*

What's funny is sometimes we think we know what we have no clue about. I thought about my worth in this way. Yes, I knew I was precious to Him, but I didn't know how much. I didn't know how much worth I was to God. I didn't know specifically the purpose and call He had on my life. With this, He revealed that everyone can't be intimate – that is, getting close and getting to know me through conversation – with me. God helped me to realize there's an uniqueness on the inside of me that draws in people, into my close quarters. So God told me I had to use clear discernment about who I spent my time with and who I give my attention to moving forward. The personality that He gave me is liked by many, but only the one would be able to handle the full me, and just not the surface level of me. As women, we hold something so valuable, that we give away freely to those who truly have no good intention for us.

God also led me to be single. And I mean single in every sense of the word! No matter that I was going on 30 years old the next year, God said, *please be single and allow yourself to breathe for a moment and get reacquainted with me.* I owed it to myself. I still had to recognize who I was. Who was Amber outside the duties of the church? Who was Amber outside the ambition of the job? Although I thought I knew who I was, I didn't really know if I did. So with all the guys who were pursuing me, I had to tell them I didn't want to start something new. It wasn't the time to carry on the hurt into the new relationship. It wasn't time to mask the reality I was single by entertaining men. I had to really sit myself down and for once start being obedient to God's instruction.

WHAT DO YOU DO WHILE YOU WAIT?

"I know what I bring to the table, so trust me when I say I'm not afraid to eat alone."

I love this quote.

When you know *what you know* about yourself, you will stop giving discounts to people, situations and especially men. You will stop allowing everyone in close quarters with you. You will start being a little selfish with yourself. You will consider yourself someone who is worth it. You will consider yourself valuable. This was where I was. I guarded my heart with all diligence (Proverbs 4:23) because I didn't want another heart quenching disaster in my life. I had to start taking care of myself in that area. I had to denounce and reject saying to myself, "Oh, this is just who I am, a hopeless romantic" and started seeing myself as God sees me. And when you get to this point, I guarantee you, you will start walking *confidently & boldly* single.

I remember looking at a TD Jakes sermon in which he explained the comparison of Gods voice to a GPS. The analogy was, when God instructs us to do something, then He expects us to do it – as like a GPS tells us when to make a right or a left. God will further direct us when He wants us to make our next move. As we tend to do with the GPS, as Jakes described, we sometimes check it to make sure it's still on and guiding us, especially when we have been riding for a long time and it seems like we are getting nowhere. So when God told me to "be single" (my first instruction after my breakup), I was quick to stick with that path for as long as God allowed me there. Yes, I received invitations to go out and received offers for dates, but I declined, for I knew I wasn't ready. Background noise from the enemy crept upon me, "*I should do this*" and "*I should date him*" and "*It's time for you to take the next step.*" I looked to God in these particular moments, *just let me know when to turn!* He always led me right back to his first instruction. Be Single.

Based on how the Lord instructed me, here are a few things to consider during this season:

God instructed me to focus on what He called me to do.

Jumping from relationship to relationship is by far the largest mistake I ever made going into relationships! I went into each one too soon, prematurely with a lot of baggage I didn't know (or even want to recognize) I had. I thought I was completely healed. I thought I was OK to move forward. But I wasn't. I wasn't OK to move forward because I was never single, let alone a Christian, to begin with! I had to find my identity in Christ. I had to know into whom was God changing me into. I had to know what were my new dislikes. What were my new likes? What career path I would be on? What ministry was I going to partake in? I needed to know who I really was *in Christ.* The same Amber that was back then chasing cheaters is not the same Amber I am today. The same Amber I am today will not be the same Amber in five more years. I desperately needed to establish myself as a Christian, wholly and completely.

Once I grasped this, the relationship fantasy grew further from my mind. I was all about pleasing God and being obedient to what He said. I learned it's so much that God wants to do in our lives outside of our destined marriage; we don't see it at times! We get so caught up on "Who it's going to be, God?" that we don't even see marriage is a small portion of our overall lives. Women, we feel like once we get married and have children, we are complete in life. But that is so far from the truth! That's only a piece of what God has promised! After marriage, guess what? We still have to answer to His call about the teaching, the ministry, the business, the mission, the evangelism and so on. There is so much God has in store for us, more to focus on than our next relationship! Working with God while we are single allows the time for us to do some of the ministry work for Him. This is why Paul said *it is better to stay single like me,* (1 Corinthians 7:8) because it's more time dedicated to the Lord and His work! Believers should be disciples in Christ, first and foremost. Before any dating, before any marriage, before any family, we are called to show non-believers the Christian walk and draw them to Him. Don't you think this mission is more important to Him than putting you in a relationship? Don't you think saving souls is more important than getting you that boyfriend?

We have to look at it like this (because we forget): We are not our own as a true Christian. Maybe in the world we think we are our own, but when you decide follow Jesus, we now are in a bigger picture of His will for our life. This is the cross we carry when we proclaim Christ in our lives. So the first relationship we have to strive for is the relationship with Christ – being with Christ prepares you for being with someone else. So during this period of building your relationship with God and recognizing your ministry calling, you have to distinctly hear His voice. To hear His voice, you have to silence other voices. This builds a relationship with God. You read Scripture every day. You pray every day. You seek Him before making decisions/reactions. When the Spirit moves you, at church take up and become a part of a ministry. Surround yourself with all things about making Jesus and Christ your No. 1 priority! When you do this, you are *watering your grass*. Some of us want to skip this step and move on to our next relationship – read a little bit of scripture, go to church and expect God to move our husband directly toward us. Relationship with Christ is most pleasing to our Savior. A Christian woman is eager to do this because she knows the importance of serving the Lord above anyone else. But what we don't see, too, we are preparing for our husband just by serving Jesus. If you don't practice serving and being submissive to the Lord, it'll be hard for you in marriage, *I'm just saying*.

The Grass is Green Where You Water It

In the season singleness, we are not called to be idle and just wait on guys to get *their* act together. We have to also water our grass and continue earnestly working on ways of improving our own lives as well. We look at relationships as if we don't have issues and weaknesses. The nagging, yes. The attitude, yes. The need for the last word, yes! You may have not been perfect in the last relationship, but that doesn't mean you can't work on improving your attributes. The past is the past, as I like to say. Your future is better. Why not also become better for your future?

Make sure your grass is lush and green, kept up with water and plenty of light (The Son).

Everything That Glitters Isn't Gold

With the example of my *last* ex-boyfriend, I was initially thrilled that he loved the Lord! That, finally, being involved with a man of faith, that attended church, knew the Bible and conducted himself as a man of God – that he righteously lead me down the aisle of our wedding. But I learned not to place so much praise on the people in the church. *Now don't get me wrong, taking the step to want to come to church and live holy is a feat in itself to do.* But I learned also not to limit myself either to the tunnel vision I once had. I was sure after having my share of cheaters and self-absorbed men, that a man who went to church would treat me right. Lesson learned: saved or not, we are all dressed up dirt in needing of a Savior every day. So my discernment quickly sharpened on the men in and outside the church. I wasn't at all impressed by *who* wanted to get to know Amber. Whether it was a pastor, singer, church goer, instrument player, or someone off the street, I really wanted someone who was absolutely real about being led every day by the Holy Spirit, and practicing walking in the fruits of the Spirit. To be led by the Holy Spirit is to be fed with it every day. I wanted to be a wife. I knew I was a wife. I wanted to try my best to exemplify all of what a Christian wife is meant to be! But I absolutely could not be submissive to someone who isn't submissive to God. To be honest, I couldn't engage in another relationship where he was not strong as, if not stronger, my Christian walk.

My relationship with God was far too precious to jeopardize. Yes, that includes men too. Getting in a relationship with the wrong man can jeopardize your relationship with Christ. It can hurt and hinder your walk *and can hurt your destiny and purpose.* Knowing my worth at that point, I didn't want just anyone coming into close proximity to me without being OK'd by God. Even what we find as a good person sometimes is not good for us: not good for us spiritually; not good for our destiny; not good for the future family. God has designed a specific plan for each and every one of us, and He knows what a guy can and cannot offer to you *in the long run.*

So ask the Lord for true discernment. My prayer all the time:

Lord block anyone and anything that wasn't sent by you to help edify me spiritually. Have those that don't mean well for my good exit out of my life, promptly. Help me to discern who I should and should not keep in my life. Help me to recognize the relationship they are supposed to have in my life. Help me not to move ahead of you. Help me to know the wolves in sheep's clothing.

That prayer right there will quickly dissolve friendships, relationships, places of employment and even family members. (So you better mean it when you pray it!) Be ready to see how quickly your nose will smell the wolves and see their motives. You will be surprised at how much more you can discern, and how more of those uneasy feelings start to happen. However, this is something you don't see within a few days or even sometimes weeks. To have true discernment you have to keep your prayer life on maximum (as you should always) and become a quiet observer. The Holy Spirit is our true helper and best friend. The Holy Spirit can provide discernment over what someone tries to hide. The Holy Spirit can let you know that man that you *think* you want that sits on the third pew in church is not the one for you. That smile and nice suit is hiding a man who isn't ready to tackle his issues of his past, and will probably end up hurting you in the long run.

Train your mind to think that everything that glitters isn't always golden.

Spend Time Alone, Please

In the marriage God has promised us, we won't have the time that we preciously have to ourselves now.

If you are like me, I can enjoy a day of getting away without the noise of the phone, emails, texts, family problems, friend problems and the like. I love "me" time. I love sitting back on a day and watching a movie without the cares of my next project or what I could be doing besides watching that movie. We have a luxury that most married couples would love to trade for a day. But they can't.

Here's why: When we marry, we join together with our spouse as one person now. So our move is our spouses move. Their move is our move. I sat back one day and was really thankful! *Yes I am single, but at least now I have some time to myself!* And I took this for granted in my single days before Christ. I was trying to find out who my boo was going to be. I was spending that time wallowing in my singleness. I wasted that alone time with randoms. I wasted that alone time crying. I wasted that alone time depressed. I didn't appreciate time to myself. I quickly opened my eyes and thanked God I had some time alone for just only me. I was trying my best in my last relationship to have time for God, my ministry, myself, friendships, work, business plans, family and then my guy. And of course, something fell short every time, most of the time it was time for only myself.

So once I got back on my feet after the break up, I thought of my time as so precious and I took full advantage of filling that time with daily meditations to God, and actually conversing with Him. I filled that time with time to just refresh – no ministry, no family, no dates, no friends and actually set some time for just me. I also watched a movie here and there. I read a book. I cooked a new dish. I tried something different. I just sometimes would lie in my bed to stare out my window. I appreciated the silence. What's so funny to me is that women who couldn't wait to get married now say " Girl, you better appreciate your time alone!" And we, as single women, think these married ladies are just giving us encouragement in our singleness. But I know it deems true if I was just in a relationship and everything was tugging on me. I couldn't imagine to what capacity it meant to be a wife!

Time alone may be scary for those who aren't sure of themselves or aren't comfortable with being single yet. I understand this struggle because the silence can seem rather loud. Being alone may not seem to have a good side. But don't get discouraged, true healing will take time. And it's best that time is spent physically alone, presently with the Lord. Everyone's healing process is different, and the time your healing will take will be different from the next girl. I believe the time it takes to completely and wholly heal is how much needs gutting out of you and the determination you have to do so. When you get to this point, however, don't allow anyone else into this space until God says move forward. The problem that many women have, including myself, is that we think we are better to move ahead and start dating someone else who we didn't consult with God first. Don't allow the enemy to trick you into thinking "It's harmless dating" because you are inviting someone into your heart to get to know you personally. Allow some time to have to yourself for a season to refresh, restore and equip you. I like Psalms 23:2-3 the amplified version: *He makes me lie down in [fresh, tender] green pastures; He leads me beside the still and restful waters. He refreshes and restores my life (my self)*. Sometimes even in our singleness we can refresh our lives, our souls and rejuvenate back what the enemy stole from us.

Because It was Done to Me

I knew what true selflessness was just by what was done to me. Our carnal reaction to being treated badly would be to retaliate on the person or to someone else. But because of the hurt and the anguish I felt, I sincerely did not want another human being to feel that low. Everything that was done to me God used it for my good! I was less self-centered. I was more selfless. I was more patient with others. I tried to end misunderstanding where there was. I avoided confusion when it was presented. I was gentler with my words when confronting someone. I was less likely to step out of a situation that I grew impatient with. Most of all, I was eager to learn in my hardships what God wanted me to learn.

There was a time my job was a little \rough and I almost was offered a job somewhere else. However, when my company needed me the most to stay, was I going to up and leave them? Just then, the Holy Spirit reminded me about how I felt when my ex-boyfriend left me high and dry. Different circumstance, yet the same type of compassion. He brought back my remembrance of everything I felt like during that time. But He told me to make a choice, to leave or stay. And as much as the circumstances surrounding the unknown for the company, I stayed. Despite what everyone thought I should do, I stayed. Because in staying, you exercise endurance, faith and trust – knowing God has already taken care of the 'unknown'. So because it was done to me, I had to prove that I could pass this test, along with many others.

So I encourage you to not allow the bad memories and the hurt cause you to hurt others. Hurt (adjective) people indeed hurt (verb) other people. Christians don't take vengeance. Christians don't use what they received to do bad. Christians still exemplify what's right and just. Christians still think on things that are lovely and of good report. Christians exercise self control and discipline. Although it hurt you, it also can help you. My bishop says the weapon that was formed against you now becomes a tool. We can either be hurt by the weapon or be strong enough to dodge what it was going to do and use it to better ourselves.

I recently saw this quote – "I know we never get over great losses; we absorb the hurt, and they carve us into different, often kinder, creatures." My personality, I know, shifted after being dumped. I totally evaluated all the things I did and did not do. I also evaluated how it made me feel. And I began to really watch over my actions on a day to day basis. Something would come up that would trigger an emotion I felt during my breakup and it allowed me to be more gracious with things. Understanding about more things. Simplistic about more things. Gentler about more things. I was more humble about things. I checked my pride when it came into the picture. So the hurt was indeed helping me. (I actually started to get a little conceited bragging on myself *whoever is the next guy to win my heart is going to be super blessed to have me!* I had to check my attitude quick.) These are the fruits we are supposed to display any way. So sometimes we have to thank our exes because of what was done to us, we can now use the hurt to show grace to someone else.

Once we know that that being single isn't being the outcast of society, we can start embracing and excelling in what season we are in right now. Most singles compare their lives to those around them, especially as we age and more and more women are becoming brides. For whatever their process was, we have to let them live out the life God destined for them. But we can't go on bypassing a season God is trying to prune us in. If we are solely dedicated to Him and dependent on Him we wouldn't mind finally listening to what He has been trying to get us to see for the longest. This takes boldness and a lot of just plainly *getting over ourselves and our immediate desires.* So many women make relationships idols, and God is trying to get us to understand there is more to this life than getting married! God is more concerned with your character, above everything.

Take my past as a stepping stone of men that you don't have to experience, or a manual for what you may now be experiencing in your own life. My 20's was not an easy road for me romantically, but necessary for the calling God has on my life. It was the ingredients I needed for my, now, husband, family and ministry and has matured me into the woman I need to be for both of them. I heard from my pastor one day in Bible study that some things are, indeed, unnecessary, but no experience is ever wasted when God has you in the palm of His hand. The reason for writing is the hopes of sharing with women that there's no fear in being single – as long as you're purposefully doing it the right way. I fully believe God knows that if you want to be a wife and have a family, He hears us. With this, He prunes us to be the best wives we can be for our future husband. Let's trust that fact!

ABOUT THE AUTHOR

AMBER RHODES is a minister, wife, mother, writer, event and travel planner, liturgical and prophetic dancer, and a former newspaper reporter. She was inspired to write *Better Left Said* "Because after being in so many dead-end relationships, I finally listened to God, healed completely from my past, and was able to move forward doing ministry allowing God to bring my husband instead of me trying to force another dead end relationship." *Better Left Said* is her debut book. You can catch Amber online at her inspirational blog *Sincerely Amber* (www.sincerely amber. net).

www.ingramcontent.com/pod-product-compliance
Lightning Source LLC
Chambersburg PA
CBHW071421040426

42445CB00012BA/1247